# OUTLIVE DIET COOKBOOK

*Transform Your Health: 1200 Days of Easy Recipes to Boost Longevity and Wellness | Complete 30-Day Meal Plan and Nutritional Tips Included*

# Table of Contents

# Introduction

This book was written from a simple but profound mission: to help you live longer and healthier. The recipes and meal plans you'll find in this book are designed to make healthful eating straightforward and enjoyable, empowering you to improve your well-being every single day.

*Our mission is simple:* to help you live a longer, healthier life through the power of nutrition. You might ask, *"Can what I eat truly affect how long and how well I live?"* The answer is a resounding yes. It turns out that food is not just fuel; it can be medicine. By choosing nutrient-dense foods, you can prevent chronic diseases, support your body's natural healing processes, and boost your energy levels—all of which contribute to longevity.

Dr. Peter Attia's research heavily influences the principles behind the Outlive Diet. He has dedicated his career to studying and understanding longevity, offering compelling evidence-backed insights into how specific dietary choices can impact our lifespan and overall health.

## The Science Behind the Outlive Diet

One of the core principles of the Outlive Diet is its foundation in evidence-based nutrition science. Numerous studies have shown that diets rich in whole foods—such as vegetables, fruits, whole grains, lean proteins, and healthy fats—can significantly reduce the risk of chronic diseases like heart disease, diabetes, and cancer.

One striking example of this can be found in populations around the world known for their longevity, often referred to as Blue Zones. These regions—areas like Okinawa in Japan or Sardinia in Italy—share common nutritional characteristics: they consume mostly plant-based diets with minimal processed foods. Their meals are rich in antioxidants, fiber, vitamins, and minerals that collectively contribute to not only a longer life but also a more robust health span.

But it's not just about what you eat; it's about how you eat too. Mindful eating is another component of the Outlive Diet that aligns with Dr. Peter Attia's guidelines. It encourages slowing down during meals to truly savor each bite, helping improve digestion and satisfaction while preventing overeating.

This cookbook makes it easy for you to adopt these principles by providing delectable recipes that are both simple and nutritious. With our 30-day meal plan included in this book, you'll have stress-free guidance on what to eat daily so you can focus on enjoying your meals rather than dreading what comes next.

In addition to recipes, you'll also find valuable nutritional tips throughout this book—covering everything from the importance of fiber and antioxidants to debunking myths around certain dietary fads.

This Introduction aims to set the stage for all that follows—the philosophy behind the diet, inspirational success stories from people like Lisa and Mark who transformed their lives through these dietary practices, practical tips for organizing your kitchen for success, simple yet delicious recipes for any meal of the day—all designed with your health longevity in mind.

We understand that adapting new eating habits is not always easy. Therefore, we've also included sections on overcoming common challenges such as finding time to cook or staying motivated long-term.

Sustainability matters here too; after all, what's good for your body should also be good for our planet. In this cookbook, you'll learn about making sustainable choices—from selecting organic ingredients when possible to reducing food waste—with an aim towards better harmony between your diet and environment.

# Why This Book Is Different

I get it—life is hectic, and sticking to a rigid diet plan can seem daunting. That's why this book is designed with flexibility and simplicity in mind. The recipes are straightforward, made with readily available ingredients, and adaptable to various dietary preferences. Whether you're a seasoned cook or a kitchen novice, you'll find these recipes easy to prepare.

One thing that sets this book apart is its focus on longevity and overall wellness. It's not just about losing weight or following the latest food trends; it's about nourishing your body in ways that can help you live a longer, healthier life. Dr. Peter Attia's principles emphasize the importance of nutrition in preventing chronic diseases, promoting mental clarity, and enhancing physical vitality.

# How to Use This Book for Maximum Benefit

To get the most out of this cookbook, start by familiarizing yourself with the foundational principles of longevity as outlined by Dr. Attia. Understanding the 'why' behind these recipes will motivate you to make lasting changes in your diet.

Next, plan ahead using the 30-day meal plan provided. This plan is structured to minimize decision fatigue and stress, offering a balanced mix of breakfasts, lunches, dinners, and snacks. The detailed shopping lists will simplify your grocery trips and ensure you have all the essential ingredients on hand.

Feel free to customize the meal plans according to your preferences and lifestyle needs. If you're short on time, you'll appreciate the quick recipes section that offers nutritious meals without requiring hours in the kitchen.

Motivation is key when it comes to long-term dietary changes. Reading success stories like Lisa's transformation or Mark's journey can inspire you to stay committed even when challenges arise.

Additionally, tips on staying motivated long-term will help you integrate these healthy habits into your daily routine seamlessly.

Don't hesitate to explore the various chapters beyond just the recipes. From budget-friendly options to gourmet dishes for special occasions, there's something here for everyone. The chapters on science-based nutrition and sustainability will deepen your understanding of how food choices impact personal health and the environment.

Remember, this isn't about perfection—it's about progress. Small, consistent changes can lead to significant improvements over time. Let's embark on this journey together toward better health and longevity.

# CHAPTER 1

## The Philosophy of Longevity

# The Concept of "Outlive": Definition and Principles

Dr. Peter Attia defines "*Outlive*" as an approach that concentrates on delaying the onset of age-related diseases and maintaining a high quality of life as we age. This concept is crucial because living longer doesn't necessarily mean living better unless we are healthy enough to enjoy those extra years. The key is to focus on preventative measures, lifestyle changes, and dietary habits that support long-term health.

In other words, "*Outlive*" isn't just about adding more years to your life; it's about adding more life to your years! It's an empowering way to think about our future, emphasizing proactive care rather than reactive treatment. Dr. Attia's approach includes practical strategies to help us outlive the typical expectations of aging by taking control of our health today.

Now that we've defined what "*Outlive*" means, let's discuss the principles that underpin this concept. Dr. Peter Attia emphasizes several core principles that guide us towards achieving better health outcomes.

1. **Nutritional Biochemistry**: Nutrition is more than just fuel; it plays a critical role in how our bodies function at a cellular level. Dr. Attia believes in tailoring nutrition based on an individual's unique biochemistry rather than following one-size-fits-all dietary advice. That means finding out what types of foods your body thrives on and making those your staples.

2. **Physical Fitness**: Fitness isn't just about looking good; it's about building strength, endurance, and flexibility that help you enjoy life and stay independent as long as possible. Each type of exercise has its own benefits:

   a) *Strength Training:* Builds muscle mass which we naturally lose with age.
   b) *Cardio:* Keeps your heart and lungs healthy.
   c) *Flexibility:* Helps maintain range of motion in your joints.

3. **Sleep Hygiene**: *Ever had one of those nights where you toss and turn?* Quality sleep is non-negotiable for outliving according to Dr. Attia. Good sleep impacts everything from hormone regulation to cognitive function and even how your body repairs itself.

4. **Mental Health**: A sharp mind is just as important as a strong body. Prioritizing mental well-being through mindfulness practices, social connections, and stress management is crucial for an outliving lifestyle.

5. **Preventive Medicine**: This principle revolves around regular health screenings and early detection strategies to catch potential issues before they become major problems.

| PRINCIPLE | FOCUS | KEY ACTIONS |
|---|---|---|
| *Nutritional Biochemistry* | Individualized nutrition | Tailored diets based on personal needs |
| *Physical Fitness* | Comprehensive exercise | Strength training, cardio, flexibility |
| *Sleep Hygiene* | Quality rest | Consistent sleep schedule, good sleep environment |
| *Mental Health* | Emotional and cognitive well-being | Mindfulness, social connection |
| *Preventive Medicine* | Early problem detection | Regular screenings |

The journey to "*outlive*" isn't about dramatic overnight changes but rather consistent daily habits that contribute to long-term health benefits. Think of it like investing – small deposits over time yield incredible results. While these principles might seem standalone now, they're actually interconnected:

- ✓ Eating well helps you perform better during workouts.
- ✓ Exercise improves sleep quality.
- ✓ Good sleep enhances mental clarity.
- ✓ Better mental health assists in making healthier choices overall.

It all ties together into one integrated approach towards outliving whatever life throws at you! In this book, we'll not only focus on recipes but also on ways these dishes can fit into your overall strategy for "*Outlive*," contributing positively to each pillar.

# Food as Medicine: Preventing Chronic Diseases

Dr. Attia has been vocal about the role of diet in keeping us healthy and preventing chronic diseases like diabetes, heart disease, and even some forms of cancer. He emphasizes not just what we eat but how it impacts our body's internal systems over the long haul.

According to Dr. Attia, one of the most significant points to understand is how different foods affect our insulin levels. High insulin levels are linked to a host of problems, including obesity and type 2 diabetes. That's why low-carb diets have become quite popular; they're designed to keep those insulin levels steady. But it's not all about slashing carbs out of our lives completely—it's more nuanced than that.

*Did you know that the food we eat can do so much more than just fill our bellies*? It can actually help prevent chronic diseases! Now, I know it sounds a bit like magic, but it's really all about the science of nutrition.

1. **The Power of Nutrient-Dense Foods**: *What does that even mean?* Well, these are foods packed with vitamins, minerals, and other nutrients our bodies need to function properly but with relatively low calories. Think leafy greens like spinach and kale, berries like blueberries and raspberries, and even fatty fish like salmon. Dr. Attia emphasizes the importance of having these in our daily diet because they provide the essential building blocks for our bodies to ward off diseases.

2. **Inflammation and Diet**: You might be wondering how eating can influence inflammation. Simply put, some foods can trigger inflammation while others can help reduce it. Chronic inflammation is linked to various diseases like heart disease, diabetes, and even cancer. Foods high in processed sugars and trans fats tend to increase inflammation. On the flip side, foods rich in omega-3 fatty acids, found in fish or flaxseeds, antioxidants from berries, and polyphenols in green tea can help decrease inflammation levels.

| ANTI-INFLAMMATORY FOODS | EXAMPLES |
| --- | --- |
| *Omega-3 Fatty Acids* | Salmon, Flaxseeds |
| *Antioxidants* | Blueberries, Strawberries |
| *Polyphenols* | Green Tea, Dark Chocolate |
| *Fiber-Rich Foods* | Whole Grains, Apples |

3. **Blood Sugar Regulation:** One thing Dr. Attia points out is the role food plays in regulating blood sugar levels. Consistent spikes in blood sugar can lead to insulin resistance over time which may progress to Type 2 Diabetes - definitely something we want to avoid! By choosing complex carbohydrates such as whole grains over simple carbs like white bread or sugary snacks, we help our bodies manage blood sugar levels more effectively.

4. **Healthy Fats Are Your Friends**: Contrary to what you might think, not all fats are bad! In fact, healthy fats are crucial for brain health and reducing the risk of heart disease. Unsaturated fats found in avocados, nuts, seeds and olive oil can improve cholesterol levels and keep your heart happy.

5. **Gut Health Matters**: *Have you ever had a "gut feeling"?* Well, there's a lot happening down there that affects your overall health! The gut microbiome is home to trillions of bacteria that play a key role in digestion and immunity. Dr. Attia recommends including fermented foods like yogurt, sauerkraut or kimchi in your diet since they introduce beneficial bacteria into your gut which can help prevent digestive issues and boost immunity.

6. **Protein's Role**: Protein isn't just for bodybuilders; it's essential for everyone! It helps repair tissues, build muscles and produce important hormones and enzymes in our bodies. Opt for lean proteins like chicken breast or plant-based options like lentils if you prefer vegetarian sources.

# The Link Between Diet and Longevity

Three years ago, top longevity physician Peter Attia, M.D., would have vigorously defended the keto diet. Today, he's taken a more nuanced approach and avoids getting caught up in diet wars.

*"The fundamental assumption underlying the diet wars, and most nutrition research—that there is one perfect diet that works for every single person—is absolutely incorrect,"* Attia writes in his new book, "*Outlive.*"

The truth, according to Attia, is that how you manipulate your diet should hinge on your individual metabolism, personal goals, and what you can realistically adhere to. *"It seems quite clear that a nutritional intervention aimed at correcting a serious problem (e.g., highly restricted diets or even fasting to treat obesity, NAFLD, and type 2 diabetes) might be different from a nutritional plan calibrated to maintain good health (e.g., balanced diets in metabolically healthy people),"* he explains.

His perspective feels refreshingly sensible. Unlike some longevity doctors who push extreme nutrition advice (often linked to profit-making proprietary diets), Attia's approach is free from such strings.

So how do you figure out how to tweak your diet for optimal health? In "*Outlive,*" Attia offers practical insights into customizing dietary changes to enhance both healthspan and lifespan, regardless of where you land on the metabolic spectrum. Nutritional needs can vary considerably based on different factors such as age, activity level, and health status. For instance:

| HEALTH CONDITION | RECOMMENDED DIETARY APPROACH |
| --- | --- |
| *Obesity* | Low-carb or ketogenic diet |
| *Type 2 Diabetes* | Controlled carbohydrate intake |
| *NAFLD* | High-protein, reduced-sugar intake |

The idea here isn't about sticking to one rigid plan but understanding what works best for you by recognizing the signals your body sends. For example:

> ➢ If you're metabolically healthy and just looking to maintain your vitality, a balanced diet rich in whole foods like fruits, vegetables, lean proteins, and healthy fats should suffice.
> ➢ On the other hand, if you're dealing with significant weight issues or diabetes, a more structured approach like intermittent fasting or a low-carb regimen might be more effective.

What I love about Attia's method is its individualized nature. You don't have to fit yourself into a dietary mold; instead, you adapt the principles to suit your life and current state of health. By understanding what your body needs nutritionally at different points in your life—and how those needs may change—you can better support long-term wellness.

To me, this is empowering. It means I have control over my health through my diet choices without having to commit blindly to one school of thought. Instead of adhering rigidly to fad diets or trends promoted by influencers or so-called experts with vested interests, I trust my body's feedback and make adjustments as needed.

# Success Stories: How the Diet Changed Lives

### Story 1: Lisa's Transformation

Lisa was always full of life and energy but over time, she began feeling constantly tired and gained a lot of weight. She tried numerous diets and workouts but nothing seemed to work in the long run. One day, she stumbled upon Dr. Peter Attia's "Outlive" book and decided to give it a try.

Lisa started with the basics; she cleaned out her kitchen, getting rid of processed foods and sugary snacks. She replaced them with fresh vegetables, lean proteins, and healthy fats. At first, it was challenging for her to adjust her eating habits, but she stuck with it.

Within a few weeks, Lisa noticed significant changes. She had more energy throughout the day and didn't experience the mid-afternoon crash she used to suffer from. Her cravings for junk food diminished as her body adapted to whole foods.

One of the biggest transformations was in her mental clarity. Lisa found that her concentration improved dramatically at work; she was no longer staring at her computer screen feeling lost halfway through her tasks. As she embraced intermittent fasting along with this diet — eating during an 8-hour window — she found herself snacking less and staying full longer.

Lisa also started tracking her progress:

> ➢ Weight loss
> ➢ Energy levels
> ➢ Mental Clarity

After three months on this diet, Lisa not only lost weight but also felt like a whole new person. Her enthusiasm for life returned, and she discovered a love for cooking healthy meals.

### Story 2: Mark's Journey

Mark had always been active growing up but when he hit his forties, he began experiencing issues with his health — high cholesterol, high blood pressure, and persistent joint pain due to arthritis. Mark was hesitant to try another "*diet*" because he thought they were all about restrictive eating or tasteless meals. But after reading several success stories on Dr. Attia's approach in the "*Outlive*", he knew he had to give it a shot.

Mark started by increasing his intake of omega-3 fatty acids through foods like salmon, chia seeds, and flax seeds while reducing his intake of sugar and grains. Similar to Lisa's journey, he incorporated more vegetables into his meals focusing on colorful combinations like bell peppers, spinach, carrots, and broccoli.

Within just six weeks:

> ➢ His joint pain significantly reduced.
> ➢ His cholesterol levels dropped.
> ➢ His blood pressure stabilized.

Mark couldn't believe the difference this diet made in such a short amount of time. Not only were his health metrics improving, but he also felt better overall. He had more energy to spend time with his family and pursue hobbies that he had neglected for years due to his discomfort.

*Both Lisa's and Mark's transformations are living proof of how the Outlive Diet can significantly impact your life. By focusing on whole foods, reducing processed sugars, and incorporating healthy fats and vegetables, they both achieved remarkable results not just in physical health metrics but in overall well-being.*

# CHAPTER 2

## Preparing for Success

# Planning and Organizing Your Kitchen

Think of your kitchen as the heart of your home and the command center for healthy eating. A well-organized space can make sticking to your diet so much easier. Here's how we can make that happen together.

Chances are, you've got a few items you never use. *Maybe an old blender or that panini press you bought on a whim?* You know what I'm talking about. Start by removing these unused gadgets. Donate them or give them to someone who might actually use them. The goal here is to have only what you really need within arm's reach.

Next up is categorizing your tools and ingredients. Trust me, this step will save you loads of time in the long run. Start by grouping similar items together. For example:

1. **Cookware:** Pots, pans, baking sheets.
2. **Utensils:** Spatulas, ladles, knives.
3. **Dry Ingredients:** Grains, pasta, flour.
4. **Spices and Herbs:** Basil, oregano, cumin.
5. **Refrigerated Items:** Vegetables, dairy products, proteins.

Here's a little tip I've found useful: store your utensils in a way that makes sense for your style of cooking. If you cook regularly, keep those often-used spatulas and knives on a magnetic strip or in a drawer close to the stove.

Now for the pantry! An organized pantry makes it so much easier to stick to any diet plan because you can actually see what you have on hand. Get some clear containers—trust me on this one—and label them. This way, when you're looking for quinoa or brown rice, it's visible right away without having to dig through bags and boxes.

| CATEGORY | EXAMPLES | SUGGESTED STORAGE |
|---|---|---|
| *Grains & Cereals* | Quinoa, Brown rice | Clear containers with labels |
| *Legumes* | Lentils, Chickpeas | Glass jars |
| *Snacks* | Nuts, Seeds | Airtight containers |
| *Baking Supplies* | Flour, Sugar | Large labeled tubs |
| *Canned Goods* | Tomatoes, Beans | Organized shelves |

Let's move on to your refrigerator and freezer next. This is one area where planning can make meal prep so much simpler! First things first: give your fridge a good cleaning out every couple of weeks. Toss anything past its prime—it's okay to let go! Allocate specific zones in your fridge:

1. **Top Shelf:** Ready-to-eat items like leftovers or prepped meals.
2. **Middle Shelves:** Dairy products and eggs.

3. **Bottom Shelves:** Raw meat and seafood (keep these lower to avoid any potential drips contaminating other foods).
4. **Drawers:** Use one drawer for fresh veggies and another for fruits.

*For the freezer:*

1. Freeze portions of pre-cooked grains or beans; these can be life-savers on busy days.
2. Label everything with dates so you know when they were stored.

One thing I love doing is planning meals ahead of time. Meal prepping can be fun if done right! Dedicating one day a week for meal prepping can make all the difference. For me, Sundays work best. I start by planning my meals for the week, taking into consideration Dr. Peter Attia's guidelines from the Outlive Diet Cookbook.

*Another critical aspect is maintaining this organization over time. It's not enough to just set it up once; you need to make small adjustments every so often to keep things running smoothly.*

# Essential Tools: Equipment and Basic Pantry Staples

Let's move on to tools of the trade. You don't need a fancy kitchen setup to be successful with this diet – just a few essential pieces of equipment will do.

1. **A Good Knife:** Invest in a sharp chef's knife and a paring knife. These are going to be your best friends in meal prep.
2. **Cutting Board:** Go for a sturdy wooden or plastic cutting board. Some people prefer having separate boards for veggies and meats to avoid cross-contamination.
3. **Blender/Food Processor:** These are fantastic for making smoothies, purees, and sauces.
4. **Cooking Utensils:** Make sure you have basics like spatulas, wooden spoons, measuring cups and spoons, whisks, and tongs.
5. **Mixing Bowls:** Stainless steel or glass bowls are versatile and durable.
6. **Non-Stick Pans:** For easy cooking and less oil use.
7. **Baking Sheets/Pans:** Essential for roasting vegetables or baking healthy treats.

Now let's talk pantry staples because having these on hand makes cooking so much easier. You don't need a lot of fancy ingredients or rare spices to eat well. Just stick to a few basics that you can use time and time again in different recipes.

1. **Healthy Fats**

    a) *Olive Oil:* Great for sautéing vegetables or making dressings.
    b) *Avocado Oil:* Another good option for high-heat cooking.
    c) *Nuts and Seeds:* Almonds, chia seeds, flax seeds – all amazing for adding texture and nutrients.

## 2. Whole Grains

    a) *Quinoa:* High in protein and extremely versatile.
    b) *Brown Rice:* A staple that'll fill you up.
    c) *Oats:* Perfect for breakfast or baking.

## 3. Legumes and Pulses

    a) *Canned Beans:* Black beans, chickpeas – super easy to toss into salads or soups.
    b) *Lentils:* Cook faster than beans and just as hearty.

## 4. Spices and Seasonings

    a) *Salt & Pepper:* Essential for almost every dish.
    b) *Garlic & Onion Powder:* Adds depth to your dishes.
    c) *Herbs like Basil, Thyme, Oregano:* Fresh or dried, these add fantastic flavor.

## 5. Proteins

    a) *Canned Tuna/Salmon:* Quick protein fix without cooking.
    b) *Eggs:* A versatile source of protein that can be cooked in numerous ways.

## 6. Fruits & Vegetables

    a) Keep a mix of fresh and frozen veggies like spinach, bell peppers, broccoli.
    b) Fresh fruits like apples and bananas are great snacks.

Here's a quick table to summarize your basic pantry staples:

| CATEGORY | ITEMS |
| --- | --- |
| *Healthy Fats* | Olive oil, Avocado oil, Nuts (almonds), Seeds (chia) |
| *Whole Grains* | Quinoa, Brown rice, Oats |
| *Legumes* | Canned Beans (black beans), Lentils |
| *Spices* | Salt & Pepper, Garlic & Onion Powder, Basil |
| *Proteins* | Canned Tuna/Salmon, Eggs |
| *Fruits/Vegetables* | Fresh (spinach), Frozen (broccoli), Fresh Fruits (apples) |

# Meal Planning Without Stress

An efficient kitchen can make a world of difference in meal preparation, helping you stay committed to your dietary goals without feeling overwhelmed. Meal planning doesn't have to be a cumbersome task. I know from personal experience that it can make life so much simpler, especially when following Dr. Peter Attia's diet principles.

Meal planning saves time and reduces stress because you never have to worry about what's for dinner. It helps you stick to healthy eating habits and reduces impulse eating.

1. **Set Aside Time Weekly:** Dedicate a specific time each week to plan your meals. Usually, weekends work best since you can also shop for groceries without rushing.
2. **Review Your Schedule:** Check your calendar to see how busy each day will be. For busier days, plan simpler meals or use leftovers.
3. **Balance Your Meals:** Ensure you include a variety of proteins, veggies, and fats as recommended by Dr. Attia.
4. **Create a Shopping List:** Write down everything you need based on your planned meals, including portion sizes.
5. **Batch Cooking:** Prepare larger quantities of food that can be eaten over multiple days or frozen for later use.

| DAY | MAIN MEALS PLANNED | SNACKS |
| --- | --- | --- |
| MON | Grilled Chicken Salad | Greek Yogurt |
| TUE | Stir-Fry Vegetables with Tofu | Nuts |
| WED | Baked Salmon with Quinoa | Apple Slices with Almond Butter |
| THU | Chicken Lettuce Wraps | Celery Sticks with Hummus |
| FRI | Cauliflower Pizza | Cheese Cubes |
| SAT | Beef Stir-fry | Berries |
| SUN | Slow Cooker Chicken Stew | Dark Chocolate Square |

# How to Stay Motivated Long-Term

Staying motivated is key when it comes to sticking with any diet plan. Here are some strategies to keep you on track:

1. **Set Realistic Goals:** Start small and gradually increase your goals as you gain confidence. For instance, begin by planning meals for two days a week and then extend it as you get more comfortable.
2. **Celebrate Small Wins:** Every step you take towards better organization and meal planning is a victory. If you successfully batch cook for the first time or follow your meal plan for a week, give yourself a pat on the back.
3. **Involve Family and Friends:** Make meal planning a group activity. Not only does this make it more enjoyable, but sharing responsibilities can also lighten the load and provide mutual support.
4. **Experiment with New Recipes:** Prevent boredom by periodically trying new recipes or incorporating different cuisines. This keeps things fresh and exciting, making you more likely to stick with the plan.
5. **Stay Flexible:** Sometimes life gets in the way of the best-laid plans, and that's okay. If you miss a planned meal or decide to order takeout instead, don't be hard on yourself. The important thing is to get back on track as soon as possible.
6. **Keep Inspiration Visible:** Post your weekly menu on the fridge or keep recipe books open to favorite dishes on the kitchen counter. Visual reminders can inspire you and make it easier to stay organized.
7. **Health Marker Tracking:** Note how you're feeling as you make healthier choices—more energy, better mood, improved digestion—and remind yourself of these benefits often.
8. **Join Online Communities:** Engaging with others who are also focused on healthy eating can provide motivation, ideas, and encouragement. There are numerous online communities dedicated to meal planning and healthy lifestyles.
9. **Create a Reward System:** Set up a reward system for yourself or your family when milestones are met, such as sticking to your meal plan for a month or trying out ten new recipes.

Remember, meal planning isn't about perfection but about creating habits that support your health goals over time. So be patient with yourself and enjoy the journey!

# CHAPTER 3

## Simple and Quick Recipes for Everyday Life

# Nutritious Breakfasts to Start Your Day Right

## 1. Energizing Green Smoothie

**Preparation time:** Five mins

**Cooking time:** N/A

**Servings:** Two

**Ingredients:**

- One cup spinach leaves
- One cup unsweetened almond milk
- One cup frozen mango chunks
- One banana
- One tbsp chia seeds
- One tsp honey (optional)

**Directions:**

1. Mix spinach, milk, mango, banana, chia seeds, and honey (if desired) in your blender. Blend till smooth. Serve.

**Tips:** Add ice cubes if you prefer a colder smoothie. Use fresh fruit if preferred, adjusting the liquid as necessary.

**Serving size:** One glass

**Nutritional values (per serving):** Calories: 150; Fat: 3g; Carbs: 33g; Protein: 3g; Sodium: 70mg; Sugar: 22g; Cholesterol: 0mg; Fiber: 5g

## 2. Overnight Oats with Berries and Almonds

**Preparation time:** Five mins + overnight soaking

**Cooking time:** N/A

**Servings:** Two

Ingredient

- One cup rolled oats
- One cup almond milk, unsweetened
- Half cup mixed berries (fresh or frozen)
- Two tbsp almond butter
- One tbsp chia seeds
- One tbsp honey (optional)
- Quarter cup sliced almonds

**Directions:**

1. In your jar or container, mix oats, almond milk, mixed berries, almond butter, and chia seeds. Stir well to mix and ensure the oats are fully submerged in the liquid.
2. Cover, then refrigerate overnight. In the morning, mix it and top with sliced almonds. Drizzle with honey if desired.

**Tips:** Mix up your toppings by adding different nuts or seeds.

**Serving size:** One bowl

**Nutritional values (per serving):** Calories: 350; Fat: 15g; Carbs: 46g; Protein: 9g; Sodium: 40mg; Sugar: 11g; Cholesterol: 0mg; Fiber: 9g

## 3. Quinoa Breakfast Bowl with Avocado and Spinach

**Preparation time:** Ten mins

**Cooking time:** Fifteen mins

**Servings:** Two

**Ingredients:**

- One cup quinoa, washed
- Two cups water
- One avocado, sliced
- One cup fresh spinach
- Two tbsp lemon juice
- Half tsp sea salt
- Quarter tsp black pepper

**Directions:**

1. In your pot, let water boil. Add quinoa, then let it simmer. Cover and cook for fifteen mins till water is absorbed.
2. Once cooked, fluff the quinoa, then divide into two bowls. Top each bowl with avocado and spinach.
3. Drizzle lemon juice over each bowl, then flavor it using sea salt and black pepper.

**Tips:** For added flavor, you can sprinkle some nutritional yeast or red pepper flakes on top.

**Serving size:** One bowl

**Nutritional values (per serving):** Calories: 320; Fat: 18g; Carbs: 39g; Protein: 9g;

Sodium: 320mg; Sugar: 1g; Cholesterol: 0mg; Fiber: 8g

## 4. Chia Seed Pudding with Fresh Berries

**Preparation time:** Five mins + overnight chill

**Cooking time:** N/A

**Servings:** Two

**Ingredients:**

- One quarter cup chia seeds
- One cup almond milk
- One tsp vanilla extract
- One tbsp maple syrup
- Half cup fresh mixed berries

**Directions:**

1. In your container, mix chia seeds, milk, vanilla, and maple syrup.
2. Cover, then refrigerate overnight till it thickens to pudding consistency. Before serving, top with fresh mixed berries.

**Tips:** Stir the chia pudding after an hour in the fridge to avoid clumping.

**Serving size:** Half bowl

**Nutritional values (per serving):** Calories: 200; Fat: 10g; Carbs: 26g; Protein: 4g; Sodium: 60mg; Sugar: 10g; Cholesterol: 0mg; Fiber: 9g

## 5. Sweet Potato Kale Hash

**Preparation time:** Ten mins

**Cooking time:** Twenty mins

**Servings:** Two

**Ingredients:**

- One large sweet potato, peeled and diced
- Two cups chopped kale
- Two tbsp olive oil
- One small onion, diced
- Half tsp sea salt
- Quarter tsp black pepper

**Directions:**

1. Warm up oil in your big skillet on moderate temp. Add diced sweet potatoes, then cook for ten mins till they begin to soften.
2. Add onion, then till translucent. Add kale, then cook for an additional five mins till wilted. Flavor it using sea salt and black pepper.

**Tips:** For a protein boost, add a fried egg on top before serving.

**Serving size:** Half portion

**Nutritional values (per serving):** Calories: 220; Fat: 10g; Carbs: 30g; Protein: 4g; Sodium: 350mg; Sugar: 7g; Cholesterol: 0mg; Fiber: 6g

## 6. Buckwheat Pancakes with Maple Syrup

**Preparation time:** Ten mins

**Cooking time:** Fifteen mins

**Servings:** Four

**Ingredients:**

- One cup buckwheat flour
- One tbsp baking powder
- One tbsp coconut sugar
- One cup almond milk
- One tsp vanilla extract
- One tbsp coconut oil (for cooking)
- Maple syrup (to taste)

**Directions:**

1. In your big container, mix the buckwheat flour, baking powder, and coconut sugar. Slowly add almond milk and vanilla, stirring till smooth.
2. Warm up non-stick pan on moderate temp and add coconut oil. Pour batter onto your pan for each pancake.
3. Cook for two mins, then flip and cook for another two to three mins till golden brown. Serve warm with maple syrup.

**Tips:** For fluffier pancakes, let the batter sit for five mins before cooking.

**Serving size:** two pancakes

**Nutritional values (per serving):** Calories: 200; Fat: 6g; Carbs: 32g; Protein: 4g; Sodium: 240mg; Sugar: 6g; Cholesterol: 0mg; Fiber 7g

## 7. Tofu Scramble with Fresh Herbs

**Preparation time:** Ten mins

**Cooking time:** Ten mins

**Servings:** Four

**Ingredients:**

- One lb. firm tofu, strained & crumbled
- Two tbsp nutritional yeast
- One tsp turmeric powder
- Two tbsp olive oil
- Salt & pepper, as required
- One-half cup chopped fresh herbs (parsley, cilantro, chives)
- One tsp powdered garlic

**Directions:**

1. In your big skillet, warm up oil on moderate temp. Add crumbled tofu, turmeric powder, powdered garlic, nutritional yeast, salt, and pepper.
2. Cook for eight mins till tofu is golden brown. Stir in fresh herbs just before serving.

**Tips:** Serve with whole grain toast or avocado slices for a complete meal.

**Serving size:** three-fourths cup

**Nutritional values (per serving):** Calories: 180; Fat: 12g; Carbs: 6g; Protein: 14g; Sodium: 180mg; Sugar: 1g; Cholesterol: 0mg; Fiber: 3g

# Light and Balanced Lunches to Keep You Energized

## 8. Mediterranean Chickpea Salad

**Preparation time:** Fifteen mins

**Cooking time:** N/A

**Servings:** Four

**Ingredients:**

- One can (fifteen oz.) chickpeas, strained & washed
- One cup halved cherry tomatoes
- Half cup cucumber, diced
- Quarter cup chopped red onion
- Quarter cup Kalamata olives, sliced
- Two tbsp olive oil
- Two tbsp lemon juice

**Directions:**

1. In your big container, mix chickpeas, cherry tomatoes, cucumber, red onion, and Kalamata olives.
2. In your small container, whisk oil and lemon juice. Pour the it on your salad, then toss gently. Flavor it using salt and pepper.

**Tips:** For extra flavor, add some crumbled feta cheese or fresh herbs like parsley or basil.

**Serving size:** One cup

**Nutritional values (per serving):** Calories: 180; Fat: 7g; Carbs: 24g; Protein: 5g; Sodium: 210 mg; Sugar: 3g; Cholesterol: 0mg; Fiber: 6g

## 9. Grilled Chicken and Quinoa Power Bowl

**Preparation time:** Twenty mins

**Cooking time:** Twenty mins

**Servings:** Four

**Ingredients:**

- One lb. chicken breast
- One cup quinoa, uncooked
- Two cups baby spinach
- One avocado, sliced
- Half cup halved cherry tomatoes
- Two tbsp olive oil
- Two tbsp balsamic vinegar

**Directions:**

1. Cook quinoa till tender, then put aside.
2. Flavor chicken breast with salt and pepper, then grill on moderate temp for six to seven mins per side till fully cooked.
3. In your big container, mix quinoa, spinach, avocado, and cherry tomatoes. Slice grilled chicken, then add to your bowl. Drizzle with olive oil and balsamic vinegar.

**Tips:** For a vegetarian version, replace chicken with roasted chickpeas.

**Serving size:** One bowl

**Nutritional values (per serving):** Calories: 420; Fat: 16g; Carbs: 36g; Protein: 33g;

Sodium: 320mg; Sugar: 3g; Cholesterol: 75mg; Fiber: 7g

## 10. Sweet Potato and Black Bean Wraps

**Preparation time:** Fifteen mins

**Cooking time:** Twenty mins

**Servings:** Four

**Ingredients:**

- Two medium sweet potatoes, peeled and diced
- One can (fifteen oz.) black beans, strained & washed
- Half cup corn kernels
- One tsp ground cumin
- One tsp chili powder
- Four whole wheat tortillas
- Two tbsp Greek yogurt

**Directions:**

1. Warm up your oven to 400°F (204°C). Toss diced sweet potatoes with cumin and chili powder then spread on your baking sheet.
2. Roast in your oven for fifteen to twenty mins till tender.
3. In your big container, mix sweet potatoes, black beans, and corn kernels. Divide the mixture evenly among tortillas then drizzle with Greek yogurt before rolling up wraps.

**Tips:** For added crunch, include some shredded lettuce in the wrap.

**Serving size:** One wrap

**Nutritional values (per serving):** Calories: 310; Fat 4g; Carbs 59g; Protein 10g; Sodium 400mg; Sugar 5g; Cholesterol 0mg; Fiber 11g

## 11. Spinach and Feta Stuffed Portobello Mushrooms

**Preparation time:** Fifteen mins

**Cooking time:** Twenty-five mins

**Servings:** Four

**Ingredients:**

- Four large portobello mushrooms, cleaned & stems removed
- One cup chopped spinach
- Half cup crumbled feta cheese
- One tbsp olive oil
- One clove garlic, minced
- One tsp black pepper
- One tsp salt

**Directions:**

1. Warm up your oven to 375°F (190°C).
2. In your pan, warm up oil on moderate temp. Add garlic and spinach, then sauté till spinach is wilted.
3. Remove, then mix in feta cheese, salt, and black pepper. Stuff the mushrooms with it. Put stuffed mushrooms on your baking sheet, then bake for twenty-five mins.

**Tips:** For added flavor, sprinkle some fresh herbs on top before serving.

**Serving size:** One stuffed mushroom

**Nutritional values (per serving):** Calories: 120; Fat: 8g; Carbs: 6g; Protein: 7g; Sodium: 320mg; Sugar: 2g; Cholesterol: 15mg; Fiber: 2g

## 12.  Zucchini Noodles with Pesto and Grilled Chicken

**Preparation time:** Twenty mins

**Cooking time:** Twenty mins

**Servings:** Four

**Ingredients:**

- Two medium zucchinis, spiralized into noodles
- Two grilled chicken breasts, sliced
- One cup basil pesto
- Two tbsp olive oil
- One clove garlic, minced
- One tsp black pepper
- Half tsp salt

**Directions:**

1. Warm up oil in your pan on moderate temp. Add garlic, then sauté for one minute.
2. Add zucchini noodles, then cook for five mins till tender. Add the grilled chicken slices to warm through. Remove, mix in basil pesto, salt, and black pepper. Serve.

**Tips:** You can make your own basil pesto or use store-bought for quicker preparation.

**Serving size:** One cup zucchini noodles with chicken

**Nutritional values (per serving):** Calories: 300; Fat: 20g; Carbs: 11g; Protein: 22g; Sodium: 400mg; Sugar: 3g; Cholesterol: 50mg; Fiber: 2g

## 13.  Tempeh and Vegetable Kebabs

**Preparation time:** Fifteen mins

**Cooking time:** Twenty mins

**Servings:** Four

**Ingredients:**

- One lb. tempeh, cut into cubes
- One cup bell peppers, cut into chunks
- One cup zucchini, sliced
- One cup red onions, cut into chunks
- Two tbsp olive oil
- One tbsp soy sauce
- One tsp powdered garlic
- One tsp smoked paprika

**Directions:**

1. Warm up your grill to moderate-high temp.
2. In your big container, mix oil, soy sauce, powdered garlic, and paprika. Add tempeh cubes, bell peppers, zucchini, and red onions to the marinade. Toss till evenly coated.
3. Thread the marinated tempeh and vegetables onto skewers. Grill the kebabs for twenty mins till tempeh is cooked through, turning occasionally.

**Tips:** You can use any mix of your favorite vegetables.

**Serving size:** Two kebabs

**Nutritional values (per serving):** Calories: 250; Fat: 14g; Carbs: 18g; Protein: 15g; Sodium: 300mg; Sugar: 6g; Cholesterol: 0mg; Fiber: 5g

## 14.  Miso Glazed Cod with Bok Choy

**Preparation time:** Ten mins

**Cooking time:** Fifteen mins

**Servings:** Four

**Ingredients:**

- Four cod fillets (about one lb. total)
- Two tbsp miso paste
- Two tbsp soy sauce
- Two tbsp honey
- One tbsp rice vinegar
- Two bunches of bok choy, halved lengthwise
- One tbsp sesame oil

**Directions:**

1. Preheat the oven to 400°F (204°C). In your small container, mix miso paste, soy sauce, honey, and rice vinegar.
2. Put cod fillets on your baking sheet, then brush with miso mixture. Arrange bok choy around the cod, drizzle with sesame oil.
3. Bake for fifteen mins till the cod is cooked. Serve.

**Tips:** For an extra burst of flavor, sprinkle some sesame seeds on top before serving.

**Serving size:** One cod fillet and one half bok choy

**Nutritional values (per serving):** Calories: 200, Fat:6g, Carbs:12g, Protein: 30g,

Sodium: 700mg, Sugar: 8g, Cholesterol: 70mg, Fiber: 1g

## 15.  Garlic Herb Roasted Pork Tenderloin

**Preparation time:** Ten mins

**Cooking time:** Thirty mins

**Servings:** Four

**Ingredients:**

- One lb. pork tenderloin
- Four cloves garlic, minced
- One tbsp olive oil
- Two tsp dried rosemary
- Two tsp dried thyme
- One tsp salt
- Half tsp black pepper

**Directions:**

1. Warm up your oven to 400°F (204°C).
2. In your small container, mix garlic, olive oil, rosemary, thyme, salt, and pepper. Rub it on your pork tenderloin.
3. Put pork on your roasting pan. Roast for thirty mins or till the internal temperature reaches one hundred forty-five degrees Fahrenheit. Let it rest for five mins before slicing.

**Tips:** Pair this dish with a side of steamed vegetables or a light salad.

**Serving size:** Four oz pork tenderloin

**Nutritional values (per serving):** Calories: 250; Fat: twelve grams; Carbs: 3g; Protein: 30g; Sodium: 500mg; Sugar: 0g; Cholesterol: 75mg; Fiber: 0g

## 16.    One-pot Garlic Broccoli And Shrimp

**Preparation time:** Ten mins

**Cooking time:** Fifteen mins

**Servings:** Four

**Ingredients:**

- One lb. shrimp, peeled & deveined
- Two cups broccoli florets
- Three tbsp olive oil
- Four minced cloves garlic
- Half tsp salt
- Half tsp black pepper
- One lemon, juiced

**Directions:**

1. Warm up two tbsp olive oil in your big skillet on moderate temp. Add garlic and cook for one minute till fragrant.
2. Add shrimp, then flavor it using salt and black pepper. Cook for four mins per side till shrimp turns pink. Remove shrimp, then put aside.
3. In your same skillet, add remaining oil and broccoli florets. Sauté for about five mins till tender-crisp.
4. Return shrimp to the skillet, then mix in lemon juice. Cook for an additional minute to combine flavors.

**Tips:** Serve with brown rice or quinoa for a complete meal.

**Serving size:** One cup

**Nutritional values (per serving):** Calories: 220; Fat: 12g; Carbs: 7g; Protein: 23g; Sodium: 550mg; Sugar: 2g; Cholesterol: 180mg; Fiber: 3g

# Simple Yet Satisfying Dinners That Make You Feel Good

### 17. Baked Salmon with Lemon and Dill

**Preparation time:** Fifteen mins

**Cooking time:** Twenty mins

**Servings:** Four

**Ingredients:**

- Two lbs. salmon fillets
- One lemon, sliced thinly
- Three tbsp fresh dill, chopped
- Two tbsp olive oil
- One tsp sea salt
- Half tsp black pepper

**Directions:**

1. Warm up your oven to 375°F (190°C). Put salmon fillets on your lined baking sheet. Drizzle olive oil, then flavor it with salt and pepper.
2. Lay lemon slices and sprinkle fresh dill evenly on your salmon. Bake for twenty mins till the salmon flakes easily.

**Tips:** Serve with a side of steamed vegetables for a complete meal.

**Serving size:** One fillet

**Nutritional values (per serving):** Calories: 320; Fat: 20g; Carbs: 1g; Protein: 34g; Sodium: 380mg; Sugar: 0g; Cholesterol: 93mg; Fiber: 0g

### 18. Stir-Fried Tofu with Vegetables and Brown Rice

**Preparation time:** Ten mins

**Cooking time:** Fifteen mins

**Servings:** Four

**Ingredients:**

- Two cups firm tofu, cubed
- Two cups mixed vegetables (bell peppers, snap peas, carrots)
- Three tbsp low-sodium soy sauce
- One tbsp sesame oil
- One tbsp olive oil
- One cup brown rice, cooked
- One tsp fresh ginger, grated

**Directions:**

1. Warm up oil in your pan on moderate-high temp. Add tofu cubes, then stir-fry till golden brown.
2. Add mixed vegetables, then stir-fry for five mins. Pour soy sauce and sesame oil into the pan, stirring well to mix.
3. Add grated ginger, then cook for another two mins. Serve stir-fried tofu and vegetables over warm brown rice.

**Tips:** Garnish with sesame seeds or green onions for added flavor.

**Serving size:** One bowl

**Nutritional values (per serving):** Calories: 290; Fat: 14g; Carbs: 28g; Protein: 15g; Sodium: 600mg; Sugar: 4g; Cholesterol: 0mg; Fiber: 5g

## 19. Vegetable And Lentil Stew

**Preparation time:** Fifteen mins

**Cooking time:** Thirty-five mins

**Servings:** Four

**Ingredients:**

- One cup lentils, rinsed
- Two cups vegetable broth
- One cup carrots, diced
- One cup celery, chopped
- One cup tomatoes, chopped
- Half cup onion, chopped
- Three cloves garlic, minced

**Directions:**

1. In your big pot, sauté onions and garlic on moderate temp till softened. Add carrots and celery, then sauté for five mins.
2. Stir in lentils, chopped tomatoes, and broth. Let it boil, then adjust to simmer. Cook uncovered for thirty-five mins till lentils are tender.

**Tips:** Add a splash of lemon juice before serving to enhance flavors.

**Serving size:** One bowl

**Nutritional values (per serving):** Calories: 230; Fat: 2g; Carbs: 40g; Protein: 13g; Sodium: 400mg; Sugar: 7g; Cholesterol: 0mg; Fiber: 12g

## 20. Grilled Shrimp with Avocado Salsa

**Preparation time:** Fifteen mins

**Cooking time:** Ten mins

**Servings:** Four

**Ingredients:**

- One lb. shrimp, peeled & deveined
- Two tbsp olive oil
- One tsp smoked paprika
- One tsp powdered garlic
- One avocado, diced
- Two tbsp red onion, finely chopped
- Two tbsp cilantro, chopped
- One lime, juiced

**Directions:**

1. Warm up your grill to moderate-high temp.
2. In your container, mix shrimp, oil, smoked paprika, and powdered garlic. Grill the shrimp for 2-3 mins each side till pink.
3. In your separate container, mix avocado, onion, cilantro, and lime juice. Serve grilled shrimp with avocado salsa.

**Tips:** For extra flavor, marinate the shrimp in the olive oil mixture before grilling.

**Serving size:** 3 oz shrimp and 1/4 cup salsa

**Nutritional values (per serving):** Calories: 200; Fat: 12g; Carbs: 6g; Protein: 18g; Sodium: 300mg; Sugar: 1g; Cholesterol: 140mg; Fiber: 3g

## 21. Baked Cod with Tomato and Basil

**Preparation time:** Ten mins

**Cooking time:** Twenty mins

**Servings:** Four

**Ingredients:**

- One lb. cod fillets
- One cup halved cherry tomatoes
- Two tbsp olive oil
- Two tbsp fresh basil, chopped
- One lemon, sliced
- Salt & pepper, as required

**Directions:**

1. Warm up your oven to 400°F (204°C).
2. Put cod fillets in your baking dish and sprinkle with salt and pepper. Arrange cherry tomatoes around the cod fillets.
3. Drizzle olive oil over the fish and tomatoes. Lay lemon slices on top. Bake for twenty mins till the fish is opaque and flakes easily. Sprinkle fresh basil over the top before serving.

**Tips:** Serve with a side of quinoa or steamed vegetables for a complete meal.

**Serving size:** One fillet (about four oz.)

**Nutritional values (per serving):** Calories: 180; Fat: 8g; Carbs: 5g; Protein: 24g; Sodium: 350mg; Sugar: 3g; Cholesterol: 55mg; Fiber: 1g

## 22. Almond-Crusted Chicken Tenders

**Preparation time:** Ten mins

**Cooking time:** Twenty mins

**Servings:** Four

**Ingredients:**

- One lb. chicken tenders
- One cup almond flour
- Two tsp paprika
- One tsp powdered garlic
- Half tsp salt
- One-quarter tsp black pepper
- Two large eggs, beaten

**Directions:**

1. Warm up your oven to 400°F (204°C).
2. In your shallow container, mix almond flour, paprika, powdered garlic, salt, and pepper.
3. Dip chicken tenders in eggs, then coat them in flour mixture. Put coated chicken tenders on your lined baking sheet.
4. Bake for twenty mins, flipping halfway through, till golden brown and cooked through.

**Tips:** For extra crispiness, turn on the broiler for the last 2 mins of baking.

**Serving size:** Two chicken tenders

**Nutritional values (per serving):** Calories: 290; Fat: 19g; Carbs: 5g; Protein: 25g;

Sodium: 543mg; Sugar: 1g; Cholesterol: 143mg; Fiber: 3g

## 23.    Greek Yogurt Marinated Lamb Chops

**Preparation time:** Ten mins

**Cooking time:** Fifteen mins

**Servings:** Four

**Ingredients:**

- One cup plain Greek yogurt
- Two tbsp olive oil
- Two tsp lemon juice
- Two garlic cloves, minced
- One tsp dried oregano
- One lb. of lamb chops
- Salt & pepper, as required

**Directions:**

1. In your container, mix yogurt, oil, lemon juice, garlic, oregano, salt, and pepper. Coat the lamb chops thoroughly with the marinade and let it sit for at least thirty mins.
2. Warm up your grill on moderate-high temp. Cook the lamb chops for five mins on each side. Let them rest, then serve.

**Tips:** For extra flavor, marinate the lamb chops overnight in the refrigerator.

**Serving size:** One lamb chop

**Nutritional values (per serving):** Calories: 280; Fat: 18g; Carbs: 4g; Protein: 23g; Sodium: 180mg; Sugar: 2g; Cholesterol: 75mg; Fiber: 0g

## 24.    Roasted Butternut Squash Soup

**Preparation time:** Fifteen mins

**Cooking time:** Forty-five mins

**Servings:** Four

**Ingredients:**

- One butternut squash (about two lbs.), peeled & cubed
- Two tbsp olive oil
- One medium onion, chopped
- Two minced garlic cloves
- Four cups low-sodium vegetable broth
- One tsp ground cumin
- Salt & pepper, as required

**Directions:**

1. Warm up your oven to 400°F (204°C).
2. Mix butternut squash, one tbsp oil, salt, and pepper, then spread on your baking sheet. Roast in your oven for thirty mins till tender.
3. In your big pot, warm up remaining oil on moderate temp and sauté the onion and garlic till translucent.
4. Add in the roasted squash and broth, then let it boil. Adjust to a simmer for ten mins.
5. Puree the soup using your immersion blender till smooth. Mix in ground cumin and adjust seasoning with salt and pepper.

**Tips:** Garnish with a dollop of Greek yogurt and fresh herbs before serving.

**Serving size:** One cup

**Nutritional values (per serving):** Calories: 180; Fat: 7g; Carbs: 29g; Protein: 3g; Sodium: 450mg; Sugar: 5g; Cholesterol: 0mg; Fiber: 6g

# Healthy Snacks to Curb Hunger Without Guilt

### 25.    Hummus with Fresh Veggies

**Preparation time:** Ten mins

**Cooking time:** N/A

**Servings:** Four

**Ingredients:**

- One can of chickpeas (15 oz), strained & washed
- Two tbsp tahini
- One tbsp olive oil
- One clove of garlic
- Two tbsp lemon juice
- 1/2 tsp salt
- Fresh vegetables (carrots, cucumbers, bell peppers, celery)

**Directions:**

1. In your food processor, mix chickpeas, tahini, olive oil, garlic, lemon juice, and salt, then blend till smooth.

2. Slice fresh vegetables into sticks. Serve hummus with fresh veggies on the side.

**Tips:** For a smoother texture, peel the chickpeas before blending. You can add a pinch of paprika or cumin for extra flavor.

**Serving size:** 1/4 cup hummus with one cup fresh veggies

**Nutritional values (per serving):** Calories: 120; Fat: 5g; Carbs: 14g; Protein: 4g; Sodium: 200mg; Sugar: 2g; Cholesterol: 0mg; Fiber: 3g

### 26.    Mixed Nuts and Seeds Trail Mix

**Preparation time:** Five mins

**Cooking time:** N/A

**Servings:** 6

**Ingredients:**

- One cup almonds
- One cup walnuts
- Half cup pumpkin seeds
- Half cup sunflower seeds
- One-quarter cup unsweetened dried cranberries or raisins
- Two tbsp chia seeds

**Directions:**

1. Mix almonds, walnuts, pumpkin seeds, sunflower seeds, dried

cranberries, and chia seeds in your big container.

2. Store in an airtight container.

**Tips:** You can add unsweetened coconut flakes for an extra crunch. Adjust the proportions based on your taste preferences.

**Serving size:** Half cup

**Nutritional values (per serving):** Calories: 220; Fat: 18g; Carbs: 10g; Protein: 6g; Sodium: 0mg; Sugar: 3g; Cholesterol: 0mg; Fiber: 4g

## 27. Apple Slices with Almond Butter

**Preparation time:** Five mins

**Cooking time:** N/A

**Servings:** Two

**Ingredients:**

- Two apples (any variety)
- Four tbsp almond butter

**Directions:**

1. Slice apples into wedges.
2. Serve each apple with two tbsp almond butter for dipping.

**Tips:** Sprinkle cinnamon on apple slices for added flavor. Use natural almond butter without added sugars or oils.

**Serving size:** One apple with two tbsp almond butter

**Nutritional values (per serving):** Calories: 200; Fat: 12g; Carbs: 22g; Protein: 4g; Sodium: 1mg; Sugar: 15g; Cholesterol: 0mg; Fiber: 6g

## 28. Greek Yogurt with Honey and Walnuts

**Preparation time:** Five mins

**Cooking time:** N/A

**Servings:** Two

**Ingredients:**

- One cup Greek yogurt
- Two tbsp honey
- One-quarter cup walnuts, chopped

**Directions:**

1. Split yogurt between two bowls. Drizzle one tbsp honey over each serving of yogurt.
2. Sprinkle one-eighth cup chopped walnuts on top of each serving.

**Tips:** You can add a pinch of cinnamon for extra flavor. Use raw honey for added health benefits.

**Serving size:** Half cup

**Nutritional values (per serving):** Calories: 210; Fat: 11g; Carbs: 18g; Protein: 10g; Sodium: 40mg; Sugar: 16g; Cholesterol: 5mg; Fiber: 1g

## 29. Baked Kale Chips with Sea Salt

**Preparation time:** Ten mins

**Cooking time:** Fifteen mins

**Servings:** Three

**Ingredients:**

- One bunch of kale, tear the leaves into bite-sized pieces
- One tbsp olive oil

- Half tsp sea salt

**Directions:**

1. Warm up your oven to 350°F (175°C).
2. Lightly drizzle the kale pieces with oil, then flavor it using sea salt. Arrange the kale on your baking sheet.
3. Bake for fifteen mins till the edges are brown, but not burnt.

**Tips:** Make sure the kale is completely dry before baking to ensure crispiness. You can add your favorite spices for an extra kick.

**Serving size:** Large handful (about one cup)

**Nutritional values (per serving):** Calories: 58; Fat: 4g; Carbs: 6g; Protein: 2g; Sodium: 170mg; Sugar: <1g; Cholesterol: 0mg; Fiber: 1g

# CHAPTER 4

## Budget-Friendly and Accessible Recipes

# Budget-Friendly Breakfasts

### 30. Banana Oat Pancakes

**Preparation time:** Ten mins

**Cooking time:** Fifteen mins

**Servings:** Four

**Ingredients:**

- Two ripe bananas
- One cup rolled oats
- Two eggs
- Half tsp baking powder
- Half tsp cinnamon

**Directions:**

1. In your blender, mix bananas, rolled oats, eggs, baking powder, and cinnamon. Blend till smooth.
2. Warm up your skillet on moderate temp, then pour small rounds of batter. Cook for two mins, flip, then cook till golden brown.

**Tips:** Add a handful of blueberries or chocolate chips to the batter for variety.

**Serving size:** Two pancakes

**Nutritional values (per serving):** Calories: 230; Fat: 6g; Carbs: 37g; Protein: 6g; Sodium: 120mg; Sugar: 8g; Cholesterol: 95mg; Fiber: 4g

### 31. Spinach Scrambled Eggs on a Toast

**Preparation time:** Five mins

**Cooking time:** Seven mins

**Servings:** Two

**Ingredients:**

- Four eggs
- One cup fresh spinach
- Two slices of whole-grain bread, toasted
- One tbsp olive oil
- One tsp salt
- One tsp black pepper

**Directions:**

1. In your container, whisk eggs, salt and black pepper. Warm up oil in your skillet on moderate temp.
2. Add spinach, then sauté for about two mins till wilted. Pour the eggs, stirring gently to scramble till cooked through.
3. Serve the scrambled eggs alongside the toast.

**Tips:** For added flavor, you can sprinkle some feta cheese over the scrambled eggs.

**Serving size:** One serving consists of two scrambled eggs and one slice of toast.

**Nutritional values (per serving):** Calories: 250; Fat: 14g; Carbs: 18g; Protein: 16g; Sodium: 400mg; Sugar: 2g; Cholesterol: 370mg; Fiber: 4g

## 32. Lemon Ricotta Pancakes with Raspberries

**Preparation time:** Ten mins

**Cooking time:** Fifteen mins

**Servings:** Four

**Ingredients:**

- One cup ricotta cheese
- One cup milk
- Two large eggs
- One cup all-purpose flour
- Two tbsp sugar
- One tsp baking powder
- Zest of one lemon
- One cup fresh raspberries

**Directions:**

1. In your big container, whisk ricotta cheese, milk, and eggs till smooth. Add flour, sugar, baking powder, and zest, then mix again.
2. Warm up your non-stick skillet on moderate temp and lightly grease it. Pour 1/4 cup batter onto your skillet, cook for two mins, flip and cook till golden.
3. Serve pancakes topped with fresh raspberries.

**Tips:** For a zestier flavor, add more lemon zest.

**Serving size:** Two pancakes

**Nutritional values (per serving):** Calories: 210; Fat: 7g; Carbs: 27g; Protein: 10g; Sodium: 150mg; Sugar: 9g; Cholesterol: 75mg; Fiber: 2g

## 33. Spinach, Tomato, and Feta Frittata

**Preparation time:** Ten mins

**Cooking time:** Twenty mins

**Servings:** Four

**Ingredients:**

- Six large eggs
- Two cups fresh chopped spinach leaves
- One cup halved cherry tomatoes
- Half cup feta cheese, crumbled
- Two tbsp olive oil
- One tsp dried oregano

**Directions:**

1. Warm up your oven to 375°F (190°C). In your big ovenproof skillet, warm up oil on moderate temp.
2. Add spinach, then cook for two mins till wilted. Add cherry tomatoes, then cook for another two mins.
3. In your container, whisk eggs and oregano. Pour it into your skillet over the vegetables. Sprinkle feta cheese evenly over the top.
4. Transfer it to your oven, then bake for about ten mins or till set.

**Tips:** Ensure you use an ovenproof skillet to transfer from stovetop to oven easily.

**Serving size:** One slice

**Nutritional values (per serving):** Calories: 180; Fat: 13g; Carbs: 4g; Protein: 11g; Sodium: 320mg; Sugar: 2g; Cholesterol: 195mg; Fiber: 1g

## 34. Spiced Apple and Flaxseed Porridge

**Preparation time:** Five mins

**Cooking time:** Fifteen mins

**Servings:** Two

**Ingredients:**

- One cup rolled oats
- Two cups almond milk
- One apple, chopped
- Two tbsp ground flax seeds
- Half tsp cinnamon, ground
- Quarter tsp nutmeg, ground
- Two tbsp maple syrup

**Directions:**

1. In your medium saucepan, let milk simmer on moderate temp. Mix in oats, then cook for about five mins or till oats begin to soften.
2. Add chopped apple, flax seeds, cinnamon, nutmeg, and maple syrup. Cook for another eight to ten mins, stirring occasionally till thickened.

**Tips:** Top with extra apple slices or more cinnamon before serving if desired.

**Serving size:** One bowl

**Nutritional values (per serving):** Calories: 250; Fat: 8g; Carbs: 40g; Protein: 6g; Sodium: 90mg; Sugar 3g; Cholesterol: 90mg; Fiber: 3g

## 35. Broccoli and Feta Frittata

**Preparation time:** Ten mins

**Cooking time:** Twenty mins

**Servings:** Four

**Ingredients:**

- One cup broccoli florets
- Eight large eggs
- Half a cup crumbled feta cheese
- Quarter cup diced onions
- One tbsp olive oil
- One tsp dried oregano
- Salt & pepper, as required

**Directions:**

1. Warm up your oven to 375°F (190°C). Steam the broccoli florets for about five mins, till they are tender but still crisp.
2. In your oven-safe skillet, warm up oil on moderate temp. Add onions, then sauté for three to four mins till translucent.
3. In your container, beat the eggs and add the steamed broccoli, crumbled feta cheese, dried oregano, salt, and pepper.

4. Pour it into your skillet, then cook for five to six mins on moderate-low temp till the edges start to set.

5. Transfer skillet to your oven, then bake for twelve mins till the frittata is fully set. Cool it down before slicing.

**Tips:** Serve warm or at room temperature. Add fresh herbs like parsley or dill for extra flavor.

**Serving size:** One slice (one-fourth of the frittata)

**Nutritional values (per serving):** Calories: 190; Fat: 12g; Carbs: 5g; Protein: 14g; Sodium: 350mg; Sugar: 2g; Cholesterol: 280mg; Fiber: 1g

## 36. Pineapple Cottage Cheese Bowl

**Preparation time:** Five mins

**Cooking time:** N/A

**Servings:** Two

**Ingredients:**

- Two cups cottage cheese, low-fat
- One cup fresh pineapple chunks
- One tbsp honey (optional)
- Quarter tsp ground cinnamon (optional)

**Directions:**

1. Split cottage cheese evenly between two bowls. Top each bowl with half a cup pineapple chunks.
2. Drizzle honey over the top if desired. Sprinkle with ground cinnamon if using.

**Tips:** Use fresh or canned pineapple in juice (not syrup) for best results.

**Serving size:** One bowl (half of the recipe)

**Nutritional values (per serving):** Calories: 160; Fat: 2g; Carbs: 20g; Protein: 14g; Sodium: 480mg; Sugar: 18g; Cholesterol: 10mg; Fiber: 2g

# Affordable Lunches

## 37.    Simple Lentil Soup with Carrots and Celery

**Preparation time:** Ten mins

**Cooking time:** Thirty-five mins

**Servings:** Four

**Ingredients:**

- One cup dried lentils, washed
- Two cups diced carrots
- Two cups diced celery
- One diced onion
- Six cups vegetable broth
- One tsp salt
- One tsp black pepper

**Directions:**

1. In your big pot, combine lentils, carrots, celery, onion, and vegetable broth. Let it boil, then adjust to a simmer.
2. Add salt and black pepper. Cover and cook for thirty mins till lentils are tender. Adjust seasoning if necessary before serving.

**Tips:** For a thicker consistency, use an immersion blender to partially blend the soup before serving.

**Serving size:** One and a half cups

**Nutritional values (per serving):** Calories: 180; Fat: 1g; Carbs: 32g; Protein: 11g; Sodium: 900mg; Sugar: 6g; Cholesterol: 0mg; Fiber: 10g

## 38.    Veggie-Packed Lettuce Wraps

**Preparation time:** Fifteen mins

**Cooking time:** N/A

**Servings:** Four

**Ingredients:**

- One cup diced bell peppers
- One cup shredded carrots
- Half cup sliced cucumbers
- One cup cherry tomatoes, halved
- Two tbsp hummus
- One tbsp olive oil
- One head of lettuce, leaves separated

**Directions:**

1. In your container, toss bell peppers, shredded carrots, cucumbers, and cherry tomatoes with olive oil.
2. Lay out lettuce leaves and spread some hummus on each leaf. Spoon the vegetable mixture onto each leaf and fold the sides over to form a wrap.

**Tips:** For extra flavor, add a squeeze of lemon juice or sprinkle some herbs like basil or cilantro.

**Serving size:** One wrap

**Nutritional values (per serving):** Calories: 50; Fat: 3g; Carbs: 7g; Protein: 2g; Sodium: 79mg; Sugar: 3g; Cholesterol: 0mg; Fiber: 2g

## 39.  Brown Rice and Black Bean Burritos

**Preparation time:** Ten mins

**Cooking time:** Twenty mins

**Servings:** Four

**Ingredients:**

- Two cups cooked brown rice
- One (15 oz.) can black beans, strained & washed
- Half cup salsa
- One avocado, sliced
- Four whole wheat tortillas
- Two tbsp fresh cilantro, chopped
- One lime, cut into wedges

**Directions:**

1. In your big container, mix cooked brown rice, black beans, salsa, and chopped cilantro together. Warm tortillas in a pan or microwave.
2. Distribute mixture evenly among the four tortillas. Top with sliced avocado. Roll up each tortilla into a burrito.

**Tips:** Serve with a wedge of lime for added zest.

**Serving size:** One burrito

**Nutritional values (per serving):** Calories: 300; Fat: 7g; Carbs: 56g; Protein: 8g; Sodium: 400mg; Sugar: 2g; Cholesterol: 0mg; Fiber: 10g

## 40.  Vegan Buddha Bowl

**Preparation time:** Fifteen mins

**Cooking time:** Twenty mins

**Servings:** Four

**Ingredients:**

- One cup quinoa
- One lb. sweet potatoes, diced
- Two cups kale, chopped
- Half cup chickpeas, strained & washed
- One tbsp olive oil
- Two tbsp tahini
- One tbsp lemon juice
- One tsp soy sauce

**Directions:**

1. Cook quinoa in your pot till tender. Warm up your oven to 400°F (204°C) and roast sweet potatoes with olive oil for 20 mins. Steam kale till tender.
2. Combine cooked quinoa, roasted sweet potatoes, kale, and chickpeas in your container. Whisk tahini, lemon juice, and soy sauce for the dressing.
3. Drizzle it on your buddha bowl, then toss gently.

**Tips:** Add a pinch of salt and pepper for extra flavor. Substitute any preferred beans for chickpeas.

**Serving size:** One bowl

**Nutritional values (per serving):** Calories: 310; Fat: 10g; Carbs: 49g; Protein: 10g; Sodium: 320mg; Sugar: 5g; Cholesterol: 0mg; Fiber: 8g

## 41. Spinach & Mushroom Quesadilla

**Preparation time:** Ten mins

**Cooking time:** Twenty mins

**Servings:** Two

**Ingredients:**

- Four cups fresh spinach, chopped
- One cup mushrooms, sliced
- Half cup vegan cheese, shredded
- Four tortillas
- One tbsp olive oil
- One tsp powdered garlic
- One tsp powdered onion

**Directions:**

1. Warm up oil in your pan on moderate temp. Sauté mushrooms for five mins till soft. Add spinach to the pan and cook for three mins till wilted.
2. Sprinkle powdered garlic and powdered onion over the mixture. Place a tortilla in a separate heated skillet, then sprinkle with half of the cheese.
3. Add half of spinach and mushroom mixture over the cheese. Top with another tortilla and cook for three mins per side till golden brown.

**Tips:** Use whole grain or gluten-free tortillas if needed. Serve with salsa or guacamole for added flavor.

**Serving size:** One quesadilla

**Nutritional values (per serving):** Calories: 280; Fat: 14g; Carbs: 28g; Protein: 8g; Sodium: 470mg; Sugar: 2g; Cholesterol: 0mg; Fiber: 4g

## 42. Grilled Portobello Mushroom Burgers

**Preparation time:** Fifteen mins

**Cooking time:** Ten mins

**Servings:** Four

**Ingredients:**

- Four portobello mushroom caps
- Two tbsp olive oil
- Two tbsp balsamic vinegar
- One tsp dried oregano
- One tsp powdered garlic
- Salt & pepper, as required
- Four whole-grain burger buns

**Directions:**

1. Warm up your grill to moderate-high temp.
2. In your small container, mix oil, vinegar, oregano, powdered garlic, salt, and pepper. Brush the mushrooms with it.
3. Grill the mushrooms for about five mins per side till tender. Toast the whole-grain buns lightly on the grill.
4. Assemble the burger by placing grilled mushrooms on the buns. Add your favorite toppings if desired.

**Tips:** You can top the burgers with avocado slices, lettuce, or tomato for extra flavor.

**Serving size:** One burger

**Nutritional values (per serving):** Calories: 211; Fat: 10g; Carbs: 27g; Protein: 5g; Sodium: 320mg; Sugar: 3g; Cholesterol: 0mg; Fiber: 4g

## 43. Turmeric Ginger Chicken Curry

**Preparation time:** Ten mins

**Cooking time:** Twenty-five mins

**Servings:** Four

**Ingredients:**

- One lb. boneless chicken breast, cut into pieces
- Two tbsp coconut oil
- One chopped onion
- Two minced cloves garlic
- One tbsp fresh grated ginger
- One tsp ground turmeric
- One cup coconut milk
- Two cups spinach leaves

**Directions:**

1. Warm up oil in your big pan on moderate temp. Add onion, then sauté till translucent. Mix in garlic and ginger, then cook for one minute. Add turmeric and cook for another minute.
2. Add chicken pieces, then cook till browned on all sides. Pour in coconut milk, then let it simmer. Cover, then cook for fifteen mins till chicken is fully cooked.
3. Mix in spinach leaves, then cook for an additional two mins.

**Tips:** Serve with brown rice or quinoa for a complete meal.

**Serving size:** One cup

**Nutritional values (per serving):** Calories: 250; Fat: 12g; Carbs: 8g; Protein: 28g; Sodium: 400mg; Sugar: 2g; Cholesterol: 70mg; Fiber: 2g

# Dinner on a Budget

### 44. Baked Chicken Thighs with Roasted Vegetables

**Preparation time:** Ten mins

**Cooking time:** Forty mins

**Servings:** Four

**Ingredients:**

- Four chicken thighs (bone-in, skin-on)
- Two cups broccoli florets
- Two cups baby carrots
- One cup cherry tomatoes, halved
- Two tbsp olive oil
- One tsp dried thyme
- One tsp dried rosemary
- Salt & pepper, as required

**Directions:**

1. Warm up your oven to 400°F (204°C).
2. Arrange chicken thighs on your baking sheet, then flavor it using salt, pepper, thyme, and rosemary.
3. Toss broccoli, baby carrots, and cherry tomatoes in olive oil, then spread around the chicken on your baking sheet.
4. Bake for forty mins till chicken is cooked. Serve immediately.

**Tips:** For crispier skin, broil chicken for an additional two mins at the end of cooking.

**Serving size:** One chicken thigh with vegetables

**Nutritional values (per serving):** Calories: 320; Fat: 18g; Carbs: 14g; Protein: 28g; Sodium: 370mg; Sugar: 6g; Cholesterol: 100mg; Fiber: 4g

### 45. Vegetable Stir-Fry with Tofu and Brown Rice

**Preparation time:** Fifteen mins

**Cooking time:** Fifteen mins

**Servings:** Four

**Ingredients:**

- One lb. extra-firm tofu, cubed
- Two cups broccoli florets
- One red bell pepper, sliced
- One cup snow peas
- Three tbsp low sodium soy sauce
- Two tbsp olive oil
- One tbsp grated fresh ginger
- Four cups cooked brown rice

**Directions:**

1. Warm up oil in your big skillet on moderate-high temp. Add tofu and stir-fry for five mins.
2. Add broccoli, red bell pepper, and snow peas, then cook for another five mins till vegetables are tender-crisp.
3. Stir in soy sauce and ginger till well combined. Serve stir-fry over cooked brown rice.

**Tips:** Press tofu before cooking to remove excess moisture for better texture.

**Serving size:** One cup stir-fry with one cup brown rice

**Nutritional values (per serving):** Calories: 350; Fat: 12g; Carbs: 42g; Protein: 16g; Sodium: 500mg; Sugar: 5g; Cholesterol: 0mg; Fiber: 6g

## 46.    Stuffed Bell Peppers with Wild Rice

**Preparation time:** Fifteen mins

**Cooking time:** Forty mins

**Servings:** Four

**Ingredients:**

- Four bell peppers, tops cut off & cored
- One cup wild rice, cooked
- One cup black beans, washed
- One cup corn kernels
- One cup diced tomatoes
- One tsp cumin
- Two tbsp chopped fresh cilantro

**Directions:**

1. Warm up your oven to 375°F (190°C).

2. In your big container, mix cooked wild rice, black beans, corn kernels, tomatoes, cumin, and chopped cilantro.
3. Stuff each bell pepper with it, then put them upright in your baking dish. Cover your dish with aluminum foil, then bake for thirty mins.
4. Uncover, then bake for an additional ten mins till the peppers are tender.

**Tips:** Use red, yellow, or orange bell peppers for a sweeter flavor.

**Serving size:** One stuffed pepper

**Nutritional values (per serving):** Calories: 200; Fat: 2g; Carbs: 40g; Protein: 7g; Sodium: 250mg; Sugar: 4g; Cholesterol: 0mg; Fiber: 6g

## 47.    Chickpea and Tomato Curry

**Preparation time:** Ten mins

**Cooking time:** Twenty-five mins

**Servings:** Four

**Ingredients:**

- Two cups chickpeas, cooked
- Two cups diced tomatoes
- One cup coconut milk
- One medium onion, diced
- Two cloves garlic, minced
- One tbsp curry powder
- One tbsp olive oil

**Directions:**

1. Warm up oil in your big saucepan on moderate temp. Add onion and garlic, then sauté till softened. Mix in curry

powder, then cook for one minute till fragrant.

2. Add the chickpeas, tomatoes, and coconut milk, let it simmer, then cook for twenty mins till thickened.

**Tips:** Garnish with fresh cilantro or lime wedges for extra flavor.

**Serving size:** One cup

**Nutritional values (per serving):** Calories: 210; Fat: 10g; Carbs: 28g; Protein: 6g; Sodium: 300mg; Sugar: 5g; Cholesterol: 0mg; Fiber: 8g

## 48. Coconut Lime Shrimp Skewers

**Preparation time:** Fifteen mins

**Cooking time:** Ten mins

**Servings:** Four

**Ingredients:**

- One lb. large shrimp, peeled & deveined
- One-quarter cup coconut milk
- Two tbsp lime juice
- One tbsp honey
- Two cloves garlic, minced
- One-quarter tsp salt
- One-quarter tsp black pepper

**Directions:**

1. In your container, mix coconut milk, lime juice, honey, garlic, salt, and black pepper. Add shrimp, then toss to coat evenly.
2. Thread shrimp onto skewers and preheat grill to moderate-high temp. Grill shrimp skewers for three mins per side till shrimp are opaque.

**Tips:** Soak wooden skewers in water for at least 20 mins prior to grilling.

**Serving size:** Two skewers

**Nutritional values (per serving):** Calories: 180; Fat: 8g; Carbs: 6g; Protein: 22g; Sodium: 360mg; Sugar: 4g; Cholesterol: 170mg; Fiber: <1g

## 49. Black Bean Tacos with Mango Salsa

**Preparation time:** Fifteen mins

**Cooking time:** N/A

**Servings:** Six

**Ingredients:**

- One (15 oz) can black beans, strained & washed
- Half cup diced red onion
- One cup diced mango
- Half cup chopped cilantro
- Juice of one lime
- Six small corn tortillas, warmed
- One-half tsp salt

**Directions:**

1. In your medium container, mix black beans, red onion, mango, cilantro, lime juice, and salt.
2. Spoon black bean mixture onto each tortilla. Serve.

**Tips:** Add avocado slices for extra creaminess.

**Serving size:** One taco

**Nutritional values (per serving):** Calories: 150; Fat: 2g; Carbs: 28g; Protein: 5g; Sodium: 330mg; Sugar: 7g; Cholesterol: 0mg; Fiber: 7g

## 50. Peanut Butter and Banana on Whole-Grain Crackers

**Preparation time:** Five mins

**Cooking time:** N/A

**Servings:** Four

**Ingredients:**

- Eight whole-grain crackers
- Four tbsp peanut butter
- Two bananas, sliced

**Directions:**

1. Spread one half tbsp peanut butter onto each whole-grain cracker.
2. Place banana slices on top of peanut butter. Serve immediately.

**Tips:** Use ripe bananas for additional sweetness. Try almond butter as an alternative to peanut butter for a different flavor.

**Serving size:** Two crackers with toppings

**Nutritional values (per serving):**

Calories: 180; Fat: 8g; Carbs: 24g; Protein: 5g; Sodium: 160mg; Sugar: 7g; Cholesterol: 0mg; Fiber: 3g

## 51. Broccoli Tots with Cheese

**Preparation time:** Twenty mins

**Cooking time:** Twenty-five mins

**Servings:** Four

**Ingredients:**

- Two cups broccoli florets, steamed and finely chopped
- One cup shredded cheddar cheese
- Three tbsp grated Parmesan cheese
- One cup whole wheat breadcrumbs
- One large egg, beaten
- Half tsp powdered garlic
- Half tsp powdered onion

**Directions:**

1. Warm up your oven to 400°F (204°C). Steam broccoli florets till tender, then finely chop them.
2. In your big container, mix broccoli, cheddar cheese, Parmesan cheese, breadcrumbs, beaten egg, powdered garlic, and powdered onion.
3. Take a small amount of your mixture, then shape it into tot-sized logs or balls. Place them on your lined baking sheet.
4. Bake for twenty-five mins till golden brown and crispy, turning once

halfway through. Serve warm with your favorite dipping sauce.

**Tips:** Make sure the broccoli is finely chopped to ensure better shaping. If you prefer a crunchier texture, you can broil the tots for an additional 2-3 mins at the end.

**Serving size:** Four tots

**Nutritional values (per serving):** Calories: 200; Fat: 10g; Carbs: 15g; Protein: 10g; Sodium: 300mg; Sugar: 2g; Cholesterol: 50mg; Fiber: 3g

## 52. Mini Caprese Skewers

**Preparation time:** Ten mins

**Cooking time:** N/A

**Servings:** Six

**Ingredients:**

- One-pint cherry tomatoes
- Eight oz fresh mozzarella balls (bocconcini)
- One cup fresh basil leaves
- Three tbsp balsamic glaze
- Two tbsp olive oil
- Pinch of sea salt & black pepper

**Directions:**

1. Thread each one of cherry tomato, basil leaf, and mozzarella ball onto each skewer. Arrange them on your serving plate.
2. Drizzle with balsamic glaze and olive oil over your skewers. Flavor lightly with sea salt and black pepper. Serve immediately.

**Tips:** For added flavor, marinate mozzarella balls in olive oil and crushed garlic for an hour before assembling.

**Serving size:** three skewers

**Nutritional values (per serving):** Calories: 150; Fat: 10g; Carbs: 6g; Protein: 7g; Sodium: 200mg; Sugar: 2g; Cholesterol: 15mg; Fiber:1g

## 53. Protein-Packed Trail Mix

**Preparation time:** Five mins

**Cooking time:** N/A

**Servings:** Four

**Ingredients:**

- One cup unsalted almonds
- One cup unsalted cashews
- One half cup pumpkin seeds
- One half cup sunflower seeds
- One half cup dried cranberries
- One quarter cup dark chocolate chips

**Directions:**

1. In your big container, combine all the ingredients.
2. Mix well to ensure even distribution. Store in an airtight container.

**Tips:** Substitute dried cranberries with other dried fruits of your choice to vary the taste.

**Serving size:** One quarter cup

**Nutritional values (per serving):** Calories: 220; Fat: 16g; Carbs: 15g; Protein: 6g; Sodium: 2mg; Sugar: 7g; Cholesterol: 0mg; Fiber: 3g

## 54.    Cauliflower Popcorn

**Preparation time:** Ten mins

**Cooking time:** Twenty-five mins

**Servings:** Four

**Ingredients:**

- One medium cauliflower head cut into small florets
- Two tbsp olive oil
- One tsp turmeric powder
- One half tsp powdered garlic
- Three fourths tsp salt
- One fourth tsp black pepper

**Directions:**

1. Warm up your oven to 425°F (218°C).
2. In your big container, mix cauliflower florets, oil and spices till evenly coated. Spread them on your lined baking sheet.
3. Roast for twenty-five mins, or till tender and slightly crisp, stirring halfway through.

**Tips:** Serve immediately while hot for best texture. For additional flavor, sprinkle nutritional yeast before serving.

**Serving size:** One cup

**Nutritional values (per serving):** Calories: 70; Fat: 5g; Carbs: 6g; Protein: 2g; Sodium: 350mg; Sugar: <1g; Cholesterol: 0mg; Fiber: 2g

## 55.    Seaweed Salad Rolls

**Preparation time:** Fifteen mins

**Cooking time:** N/A

**Servings:** Four

**Ingredients:**

- Two cups mixed seaweed
- One cup thinly sliced cucumber
- Half a cup carrots, julienned
- One ripe thinly sliced avocado
- Two tbsp rice vinegar
- Two tbsp soy sauce (low sodium)
- Four sheets of nori

**Directions:**

1. In your container, mix seaweed with rice vinegar and soy sauce. Put one sheet of nori on your flat surface.
2. Arrange some cucumber, carrot, avocado slices, and a portion of the seasoned seaweed on one end.
3. Roll the nori tightly around the filling to make a roll. Repeat for the remaining three sheets of nori.

**Tips:** Serve with additional soy sauce or your favorite dipping sauce.

**Serving size:** 1 roll

**Nutritional values (per serving):** Calories: 70; Fat: 3g; Carbs: 7g; Protein: 2g; Sodium: 320mg; Sugar: 1g; Cholesterol: 0mg; Fiber: 3g

# 56.    Spiced Pumpkin Seeds

**Preparation time:** Five mins

**Cooking time:** Twenty mins

**Servings:** Four

**Ingredients:**

- One cup raw pumpkin seeds
- One tbsp olive oil
- One tsp paprika
- Half tsp cumin powder
- Half tsp salt
- Quarter tsp cayenne pepper

**Directions:**

1. Warm up your oven to 350°F (175°C).
2. In your container, mix pumpkin seeds, oil and spices till evenly coated. Spread seeds on your baking sheet.
3. Bake for twenty mins, stirring occasionally, till crispy.

**Tips:** Let the seeds cool before serving for extra crunchiness.

**Serving size:** Quarter cup

**Nutritional values (per serving):** Calories: 180; Fat: 16g; Carbs: 4g; Protein: 8g; Sodium: 150mg; Sugar: 0g; Cholesterol: 0mg; Fiber: 2g

# Low-Cost Desserts

## 57.  Baked Cinnamon Apples with Oats

**Preparation time:** Ten mins

**Cooking time:** Twenty-five mins

**Servings:** Four

**Ingredients:**

- Four apples, cored & sliced thinly
- One cup rolled oats
- Two tbsp honey
- One tsp cinnamon
- Two tbsp melted butter
- One-fourth cup chopped walnuts (optional)
- One-fourth cup raisins (optional)

**Directions:**

1. Warm up your oven to 350°F (175°C). Put apples in your baking dish.
2. In your container, mix oats, honey, cinnamon, melted butter, walnuts, and raisins if using.
3. Spread the oat mixture evenly over the apple slices. Bake for twenty-five mins or till apples are tender and oats are golden.

**Tips:** For added flavor, sprinkle a pinch of nutmeg. Serve with a dollop of Greek yogurt for extra creaminess.

**Serving size:** One serving

**Nutritional values (per serving):** Calories: 210; Fat: 6g; Carbs: 38g; Protein: 3g; Sodium: 5mg; Sugar: 20g; Cholesterol: 7mg; Fiber: 4g

## 58.  No-Bake Coconut Macaroons

**Preparation time:** Ten mins

**Cooking time:** N/A

**Servings:** Twelve

**Ingredients:**

- One and a half cups unsweetened shredded coconut
- One-fourth cup almond flour
- One-third cup pure maple syrup
- Two tbsp coconut oil, melted
- One tsp vanilla extract
- A pinch of sea salt

**Directions:**

1. In your big container, mix shredded coconut, almond flour, and sea salt. Add maple syrup, coconut oil, and vanilla.
2. Mix till well combined and the mixture holds together. Using a tablespoon or cookie scoop, form small balls, then put them on your lined baking sheet.
3. Chill in your refrigerator for at least thirty mins before serving.

**Tips:** For added flavor, you can dip each macaroon into melted dark chocolate.

**Serving size:** 1 macaroon

**Nutritional values (per serving):** Calories: 105; Fat: 9g; Carbs: 6g; Protein: 1g; Sodium: 25mg; Sugar: 5g; Cholesterol: 0mg; Fiber: 2g

## 59.      Gluten-Free Carrot Cake Muffins

**Preparation time:** Fifteen mins

**Cooking time:** Twenty mins

**Servings:** Twelve

**Ingredients:**

- One and one-fourth cups almond flour
- Half cup grated carrots
- One-third cup pure maple syrup
- Two eggs, beaten
- One tsp ground cinnamon
- Half tsp baking soda
- One-eighth tsp sea salt

**Directions:**

1. Warm up your oven to 350°F (175°C), then line your muffin tin with paper liners.
2. In your container, mix almond flour, ground cinnamon, baking soda, and sea salt. Add carrots, beaten eggs, and maple syrup. Mix well.
3. Spoon the batter into your muffin liners, then bake for twenty mins. Cool it down, then serve.

**Tips:** You can add chopped nuts or raisins if desired (optional).

**Serving size:** 1 muffin

**Nutritional values (per serving):** Calories: 130; Fat: 9g; Carbs: 9g; Protein: 3g; Sodium: 95mg; Sugar: 6g; Cholesterol: 40mg; Fiber: 2g

## 60.      Pistachio and Rosewater Nice Cream

**Preparation time:** Ten mins + freezing time

**Cooking time:** N/A

**Servings:** Four

**Ingredients:**

- Two ripe bananas, frozen and sliced
- One-fourth cup pistachios, shelled
- One tbsp rosewater
- One tbsp maple syrup
- One-third cup full-fat coconut milk

**Directions:**

1. In your food processor, blend the frozen banana slices till creamy. Add the pistachios, rosewater, maple syrup, and coconut milk.
2. Blend till smooth and well combined. Transfer it to your loaf pan and freeze for at least four hours. Scoop and serve.

**Tips:** Garnish with chopped pistachios for extra crunch.

**Serving size:** Half cup

**Nutritional values (per serving):** Calories: 150; Fat: 5g; Carbs: 20g; Protein: 2g; Sodium: 0mg; Sugar: 12g; Cholesterol: 0mg; Fiber: 3g

## 61. Dairy-Free Strawberry Cheesecake Bites

**Preparation time:** Fifteen mins + freezing time

**Cooking time:** N/A

**Servings:** Eight

**Ingredients:**

- One cup fresh strawberries
- One cup raw cashews, soaked overnight
- Three tbsp coconut oil, melted
- Two tbsp lemon juice
- One-fourth cup maple syrup
- One tsp vanilla extract

**Directions:**

1. In your blender, mix cashews, strawberries, coconut oil, lemon juice, maple syrup, and vanilla. Blend till smooth.
2. Pour the mixture into mini muffin molds or an ice cube tray. Freeze for at least two hours. Serve.

**Tips:** Garnish with sliced strawberries or a sprinkle of crushed cashews.

**Serving size:** One bite

**Nutritional values (per serving):** Calories: 100; Fat: 7g; Carbs: 9g; Protein: 3g; Sodium: 0mg; Sugar: 5g; Cholesterol: 0mg; Fiber: 1g

## 62. Hazelnut Mocha Protein Bars

**Preparation time:** Fifteen mins

**Cooking time:** N/A

**Servings:** Eight

**Ingredients:**

- Two cups rolled oats
- One cup protein powder (mocha flavor)
- One-half cup hazelnuts, chopped
- One-half cup almond butter
- One-quarter cup honey
- One-quarter cup almond milk, unsweetened
- One tsp vanilla extract

**Directions:**

1. In your big container, mix rolled oats, protein powder, and chopped hazelnuts.
2. In another container, mix almond butter, honey, almond milk, and vanilla extract till smooth. Combine it with oat mixture till blended.
3. Press it into your lined baking dish and refrigerate for at least one hour. Slice into bars, then serve.

**Tips:** Store in your airtight container in the refrigerator for up to one week.

**Serving size:** One bar

**Nutritional values (per serving):** Calories: 250; Fat: 14g; Carbs: 22g; Protein: 10g; Sodium: 75mg; Sugar: 10g; Cholesterol: 0mg; Fiber: 4g

# CHAPTER 5

## Gourmet Recipes for Special Occasions

## 63. Avocado and Mango Salad with Lime Dressing

**Preparation time:** Fifteen mins

**Cooking time:** N/A

**Servings:** Four

**Ingredients:**

- Two ripe avocados, cubed
- Two ripe mangoes, cubed
- One-fourth cup chopped red onion
- One-fourth cup fresh cilantro, chopped
- Two tbsp lime juice
- One tbsp olive oil
- Salt to taste

**Directions:**

1. In your big container, mix avocado, mango, onion, and cilantro.
2. In your small container, whisk lime juice, oil, and salt. Drizzle it on your salad and toss gently. Serve.

**Tips:** For extra crunch, add a handful of chopped nuts like almonds or cashews.

**Serving size:** One serving

**Nutritional values (per serving):** Calories: 220; Fat: 15g; Carbs: 23g; Protein: 2g; Sodium: 120mg; Sugar: 14g; Cholesterol: 0mg; Fiber: 7g

## 64. Edamame Hummus with Veggie Sticks

**Preparation time:** Twenty mins

**Cooking time:** N/A

**Servings:** Four

**Ingredients:**

- One and a half cups shelled edamame, cooked
- One quarter cup tahini
- One quarter cup lemon juice
- Two minced cloves garlic
- One half tsp salt
- Three tbsp olive oil
- One quarter cup water

**Directions:**

1. In your food processor, mix edamame, tahini, lemon juice, garlic, and salt.
2. Blend till smooth, gradually adding the olive oil and water to reach desired consistency. Transfer to a serving bowl.

**Tips:** Serve with an assortment of fresh veggie sticks such as carrot sticks, cucumber slices, and bell pepper strips.

**Serving size:** One quarter cup hummus with veggie sticks

**Nutritional values (per serving):** Calories: 160; Fat: 10g; Carbs: 12g; Protein: 6g; Sodium: 200mg; Sugar: 1g; Cholesterol: 0mg; Fiber: 4g

## 65.   Avocado Deviled Eggs

**Preparation time:** Fifteen mins

**Cooking time:** N/A

**Servings:** Eight

**Ingredients:**

- Four large eggs, hard-boiled, peeled, sliced in half lengthwise & yolks removed
- One ripe avocado, peeled and pitted
- Two tbsp Greek yogurt
- One tbsp lime juice
- One minced clove garlic
- One half tsp salt
- Pinch of paprika for garnish

**Directions:**

1. In your container, mash the avocado with yogurt, lime juice, garlic, and salt till smooth.
2. Spoon or pipe the avocado mixture into your egg white halves. Sprinkle with paprika for garnish.

**Tips:** For an added kick, mix in a little hot sauce to the avocado mixture.

**Serving size:** Two halves

**Nutritional values (per serving):** Calories: 75; Fat: 6g; Carbs: 3g; Protein: 4g; Sodium: 180mg; Sugar: 0g; Cholesterol: 105mg; Fiber: 2g

## 66.   Spicy Roasted Chickpeas

**Preparation time:** Ten mins

**Cooking time:** Thirty mins

**Servings:** Four

**Ingredients:**

- Two cups cooked chickpeas, washed, strained & dried
- Two tbsp olive oil
- One tsp paprika
- One half tsp cayenne pepper
- One tsp powdered garlic
- Three fourths tsp salt

**Directions:**

1. Warm up your oven to 400°F (204°C). In your container, mix chickpeas, oil and spices till blended.
2. Spread chickpeas on your baking sheet. Roast for thirty mins, stirring halfway through for even cooking.

**Tips:** Allow chickpeas to cool completely for maximum crunchiness. Adjust the spiciness by modifying the amount of cayenne pepper.

**Serving size:** Half cup

**Nutritional values (per serving):** Calories: 180; Fat: 7g; Carbs: 24g; Protein: 6g; Sodium: 350mg; Sugar: 1g; Cholesterol: 0mg; Fiber: 5g

## 67.  Smoked Salmon Canapés with Dill and Capers

**Preparation time:** Ten mins

**Cooking time:** N/A

**Servings:** Eight

**Ingredients:**

- Eight oz smoked salmon slices
- Four oz cream cheese
- Two tbsp capers
- One tbsp fresh dill
- Three tbsp lemon juice
- Eight whole grain crackers

**Directions:**

1. Spread some cream cheese on each cracker. Top each with a smoked salmon slice. Sprinkle capers evenly over the salmon-topped crackers.
2. Drizzle lemon juice lightly over each canapé. Garnish with fresh dill sprigs on top.

**Tips:** Serve chilled for best flavor.

**Serving size:** One canapé

**Nutritional values (per serving):** Calories: 100; Fat: 7g; Carbs: 5g; Protein: 6g; Sodium: 200mg; Sugar: 1g; Cholesterol: 20mg; Fiber: 1g

## 68.  Herb-Roasted Cashews

**Preparation time:** Five mins

**Cooking time:** Fifteen mins

**Servings:** Four

**Ingredients:**

- Two cups raw cashews
- One tbsp olive oil
- One tsp dried rosemary
- One tsp dried thyme
- One tsp sea salt
- Half tsp black pepper

**Directions:**

1. Warm up your oven to 350°F (175°C).
2. In your big container, toss the cashews with olive oil, rosemary, thyme, sea salt, and pepper till evenly coated.
3. Spread the cashews on your baking sheet. Roast for fifteen mins, stirring every five mins for even cooking.

**Tips:** Store leftover cashews in an airtight container. You can substitute other favorite herbs.

**Serving size:** Half cup

**Nutritional values (per serving):** Calories: 200; Fat: 16g; Carbs: 12g; Protein: 6g; Sodium: 150mg; Sugar: 1g; Cholesterol: 0mg; Fiber: 2g

## 69.  Carrot and Ginger Soup Shooters

**Preparation time:** Ten mins

**Cooking time:** Twenty-five mins

**Servings:** Four

**Ingredients:**

- One lb. carrots, peeled and chopped
- One medium chopped onion
- Two minced cloves garlic
- One tbsp olive oil

- Two cups vegetable broth
- One inch piece fresh grated ginger
- Half tsp sea salt

**Directions:**

1. In your big pot, warm up oil on moderate temp. Add onion, cook for five mins till soft and translucent.
2. Add garlic and ginger, then cook for one more minute till fragrant. Add the carrots and vegetable broth to the pot.
3. Let it boil, then simmer for twenty mins or till carrots are tender. Puree the soup using your immersion blender till smooth. Flavor it with sea salt.

**Tips:** Serve hot or chilled depending on preference. Garnish with fresh herbs for extra flavor.

**Serving size:** Half cup

**Nutritional values (per serving):** Calories: 90; Fat: 4g; Carbs: 12g; Protein: 1g; Sodium: 400mg; Sugar: 6g; Cholesterol: 0mg; Fiber: 3g

## 70. Herb-Crusted Roast Chicken with Root Vegetables

**Preparation time:** Fifteen mins

**Cooking time:** One hour and ten mins

**Servings:** Four

**Ingredients:**

- One whole chicken (about four lb.)
- Two cups baby carrots
- Three cups quartered potatoes
- One cup chopped onions
- Two tbsp olive oil
- Two tbsp mixed fresh herbs (rosemary, thyme, parsley)
- One tsp salt
- Half tsp black pepper

**Directions:**

1. Warm up your oven to 400°F (204°C).
2. In your small container, mix herbs, salt, and black pepper. Rub olive oil all on your chicken, then coat it with the herb mixture.
3. Put chicken in your roasting pan and surround it with the carrots, potatoes, and onions.
4. Roast for one hour and ten mins or till the internal temperature reaches one hundred sixty-five degrees Fahrenheit. Cool it down before carving.

**Tips:** You can add garlic cloves for extra flavor. Baste the chicken with its own juices halfway through cooking for a crispier skin.

**Serving size:** One-quarter of chicken with vegetables

**Nutritional values (per serving):** Calories: 450; Fat: 22g; Carbs: 20g; Protein: 40g; Sodium: 600mg; Sugar: 5g; Cholesterol: 110mg; Fiber: 4g

## 71. Stuffed Portobello Mushrooms with Quinoa and Spinach

**Preparation time:** Twenty mins

**Cooking time:** Thirty mins

**Servings:** Four

**Ingredients:**

- Four big portobello mushrooms, stems removed
- One cup cooked quinoa
- Two cups fresh spinach leaves, chopped
- Half cup diced tomatoes

- Two tbsp olive oil
- One tsp powdered garlic
- Half tsp salt
- Quarter tsp black pepper

**Directions:**

1. Warm up your oven to 375°F (191°C). Brush mushrooms with one tbsp olive oil.
2. In your container, mix quinoa, spinach, tomatoes, powdered garlic, salt, and pepper. Stuff each mushroom cap with it.
3. Put stuffed mushrooms on your lined baking sheet; drizzle remaining oil over them. Bake for about twenty to twenty-five mins till tender.

**Tips:** Top with a sprinkle of nutritional yeast before serving for a cheesy flavor.

**Serving size:** One stuffed mushroom cap

**Nutritional values (per serving):** Calories: 180; Fat: 8g; Carbs: 18g; Protein: 6g; Sodium: 400mg; Sugar: 3g; Cholesterol: 0mg; Fiber: 4g

## 72.    Grilled Lamb Chops with Rosemary and Garlic

**Preparation time:** Ten mins

**Cooking time:** Fifteen mins

**Servings:** Four

**Ingredients:**

- Four lamb chops
- Two tbsp fresh rosemary, chopped
- Three cloves garlic, minced
- Two tbsp olive oil
- One tsp salt
- One tsp black pepper

**Directions:**

1. In your small container, mix rosemary, garlic, olive oil, salt, and black pepper. Rub it all over the lamb chops.
2. Warm up your grill to moderate-high temp. Put lamb chops on your grill, then cook for six to seven mins per side. Let it rest before serving.

**Tips:** For extra flavor, marinate the lamb chops in the rosemary-garlic mixture for up to one hour before grilling.

**Serving size:** One lamb chop

**Nutritional values (per serving):** Calories: 250; Fat: 18g; Carbs: 1g; Protein: 21g; Sodium: 300mg; Sugar: 0g; Cholesterol: 70mg; Fiber: 0g

## 73.    Seared Scallops with Lemon Butter Sauce

**Preparation time:** Ten mins

**Cooking time:** Ten mins

**Servings:** Four

**Ingredients:**

- One lb. sea scallops, pat dried
- Two tbsp olive oil
- Three tbsp butter, divided
- One lemon, juiced and zested
- Two cloves garlic, minced
- One tbsp chopped parsley
- One pinch salt
- One pinch black pepper

**Directions:**

1. Flavor scallops with salt and pepper. Warm up two tbsp oil in your big skillet on moderate-high temp.
2. Add scallops, then sear for two to three mins per side till golden brown. Remove scallops, then put aside.
3. In your same skillet, add two tbsp butter, garlic, lemon juice, and zest, then cook for one minute till fragrant.
4. Add scallops, then spoon the sauce over them while cooking for an additional minute. Garnish with fresh parsley before serving.

**Tips:** Do not overcrowd the skillet when searing scallops to ensure a great sear.

**Serving size:** Four ounces of scallops

**Nutritional values (per serving):** Calories: 220; Fat: 16g; Carbs: 3g; Protein: 17g; Sodium: 300mg; Sugar: 1g; Cholesterol: 50mg; Fiber: <1g

## 74. Sweet Potato and Black Bean Chili

**Preparation time:** Fifteen mins

**Cooking time:** Thirty mins

**Servings:** Four

**Ingredients:**

- Two cups peeled and diced sweet potatoes
- One tbsp olive oil
- One tsp minced garlic
- One cup diced onion
- One tsp ground cumin
- One tsp chili powder
- Two cups black beans (cooked or canned)
- Two cups vegetable broth

**Directions:**

1. In your big pot, warm up oil on moderate temp. Add garlic and onion, cooking till softened.
2. Mix in cumin and chili powder. Add sweet potatoes, then cook for five mins. Pour in broth, then let it boil.
3. Cover, then simmer for twenty mins till sweet potatoes are tender. Add the black beans and simmer for another five mins.

**Tips:** For a spicier chili, add a pinch of cayenne pepper. Garnish with fresh cilantro or avocado slices.

**Serving size:** One cup

**Nutritional values (per serving):** Calories: 200; Fat: 3g; Carbs: 38g; Protein: 7g; Sodium: 400mg; Sugar: 7g; Cholesterol: 0mg; Fiber: 11g

## 75. Tofu and Broccoli Stir-Fry

**Preparation time:** Ten mins

**Cooking time:** Fifteen mins

**Servings:** Four

**Ingredients:**

- One lb. firm tofu, cubed
- Two cups broccoli florets
- Two tbsp low sodium soy sauce
- One tbsp sesame oil
- One tsp minced garlic
- One tsp grated ginger
- A half cup sliced bell peppers
- A quarter cup water

**Directions:**

1. Warm up sesame oil in your big pan on moderate temp. Add garlic and ginger, then sauté till fragrant.
2. Add cubed tofu and cook till golden brown. Add broccoli florets and sliced bell peppers, then cook for five mins.
3. Stir in the soy sauce and a quarter cup water. Cover and steam for additional five mins.

**Tips:** Sprinkle with sesame seeds before serving for added texture.

**Serving size:** One cup

**Nutritional values (per serving):** Calories: 180; Fat: 10g; Carbs: 12g; Protein: 14g; Sodium: 300mg; Sugar: 3g; Cholesterol: 0mg; Fiber: 4g

# Desserts That Make You Feel Good Without the Guilt

## 76.  Dark Chocolate Avocado Mousse

**Preparation time:** Ten mins

**Cooking time:** N/A

**Servings:** Four

**Ingredients:**

- Two ripe avocados
- One-quarter cup unsweetened cocoa powder
- One-quarter cup maple syrup
- Two tbsp almond milk
- One tsp vanilla extract

**Directions:**

1. In a blender, mix avocados, cocoa, maple syrup, milk, and vanilla. Blend till smooth.
2. Divide the mixture into four serving glasses. Refrigerate for at least one hour before serving.

**Tips:** Garnish with fresh berries or nuts for added texture and flavor.

**Serving size:** Half cup

**Nutritional values (per serving):** Calories: 190; Fat: 14g; Carbs: 18g; Protein: 2g; Sodium: 10mg; Sugar: 9g; Cholesterol: 0mg; Fiber: 8g

## 77.  Chia Pudding with Mango and Coconut

**Preparation time:** Ten mins + overnight refrigeration

**Cooking time:** N/A

**Servings:** Four

**Ingredients:**

- One cup chia seeds
- Two cups coconut milk
- One tbsp maple syrup
- One tsp vanilla extract
- One ripe mango, diced
- Two tbsp shredded coconut

**Directions:**

1. In your container, mix chia seeds, milk, maple syrup, and vanilla. Mix well to combine and ensure there are no lumps.
2. Refrigerate overnight or for at least four hours till it achieves a pudding-like consistency. Before serving, top with diced mango and shredded coconut.

**Tips:** Use ripe mangoes for the best sweetness and flavor.

**Serving size:** One cup

**Nutritional values (per serving):** Calories: 250; Fat: 15g; Carbs: 26g; Protein: 5g; Sodium: 40mg; Sugar: 16g; Cholesterol: 0mg; Fiber: 11g

## 78. Almond Flour Chocolate Cake with Raspberries

**Preparation time:** Fifteen mins

**Cooking time:** Twenty-five mins

**Servings:** 8

**Ingredients:**

- Two cups almond flour
- Half cup unsweetened cocoa powder
- Three large eggs
- Half cup maple syrup
- One tsp baking powder
- One tsp vanilla extract
- One cup fresh raspberries

**Directions:**

1. Warm up your oven to 350°F (175°C). Grease an 8-inch round cake pan.
2. In your container, whisk flour, cocoa, and baking powder.
3. In another bowl, beat eggs, then add the maple syrup and vanilla extract. Combine it with flour mixture till blended. Fold in half of the raspberries into the batter.
4. Pour the batter into the prepared cake pan and scatter remaining raspberries on top. Bake for about twenty-five mins. Cool it down, then serve.

**Tips:** Serve with a dollop of coconut whipped cream for added indulgence.

**Serving size:** One slice

**Nutritional values (per serving):** Calories: 200; Fat: 16g; Carbs: 18g; Protein: 6g; Sodium: 95mg; Sugar: 11g; Cholesterol: 55mg; Fiber: 4g

## 79. Vegan Pumpkin Spice Energy Balls

**Preparation time:** Ten mins

**Cooking time:** N/A

**Servings:** Twelve

**Ingredients:**

- One cup pitted dates
- One cup rolled oats
- One-half cup canned pumpkin puree
- Two tbsp chia seeds
- Two tbsp maple syrup
- One tsp pumpkin spice mix
- One-half tsp vanilla extract

**Directions:**

1. In your food processor, blend dates till they form a thick paste.
2. Add rolled oats, pumpkin puree, chia seeds, maple syrup, pumpkin spice, and vanilla. Blend till well combined. Roll it into bite-sized balls using your hands.
3. Refrigerate for at least thirty mins before serving.

**Tips:** Keep in an airtight container in the fridge for up to one week or freeze for longer storage.

**Serving size:** One ball

**Nutritional values (per serving):** Calories: 90; Fat: 2g; Carbs: 18g; Protein: 2g; Sodium: 5mg; Sugar: 12g; Cholesterol: 0mg; Fiber: 3g

## 80. Low-Carb Cinnamon Roll Mug Cake

**Preparation time:** Five mins

**Cooking time:** One min

**Servings:** One

**Ingredients:**

- Two tbsp almond flour
- One tbsp coconut flour
- One tbsp granulated sweetener of choice
- Half tsp baking powder
- One egg
- Two tbsp unsweetened almond milk
- Half tsp cinnamon
- Quarter tsp vanilla extract

**Directions:**

1. In your microwave-safe mug or ramekin, mix almond flour, coconut flour, granulated sweetener, and baking powder.
2. Add the egg, unsweetened almond milk, cinnamon, and vanilla and stir till well combined. Microwave on high for one minute or till cooked through.

**Tips:** For a richer flavor, you can add a dollop of sugar-free cream cheese frosting on top.

**Serving size:** One mug cake

**Nutritional values (per serving):** Calories: 170; Fat: 12g; Carbs: 6g; Protein: 8g; Sodium: 170mg; Sugar: <1g; Cholesterol: 185mg; Fiber: 3g

# CHAPTER 6

## 30-Day Meal Plan

# Structure of the 30-Day Meal Plan

This meal plan is a month-long journey towards better health and well-being. It's not just about losing weight; it's designed to improve your overall vitality and longevity. We break down the month into weeks for easy navigation and smaller, manageable milestones.

**Week 1: Detox and Cleanse**

*Aim:* To rid your body of toxins and "reset" your system.

*Focus:* High intake of fruits, vegetables, whole grains, and ample hydration.

**Week 2: Stabilize Blood Sugar**

*Aim:* To balance blood sugar levels.

*Focus:* Low-GI (Glycemic Index) foods like legumes, lean proteins, and fibrous veggies.

**Week 3: Nutrient Optimization**

*Aim:* To ensure you're getting a full spectrum of vitamins and minerals.

*Focus:* Diverse food groups including nuts, seeds, lean meats, dairy alternatives, and fermented foods.

**Week 4: Sustainable Eating**

*Aim:* To form sustainable eating habits that you can continue post the plan.

*Focus:* A balanced diet that incorporates all previously emphasized elements but in a more relaxed fashion.

## Goals of the Meal Plan

Our goals revolve around three primary aspects:

1. **Physical Health Improvements**

   ➤ Noticeable reductions in weight.
   ➤ Improved digestion and gut health.
   ➤ Enhanced energy levels.

2. **Mental Clarity & Emotional Well-being**

   ➤ Better focus and cognitive function through balanced nutrition.
   ➤ Reduced stress levels thanks to mindful eating practices.

3. **Longevity & Disease Prevention**

   ➤ Adopting an anti-inflammatory diet to ward off chronic diseases.
   ➤ Improving metabolic health to enhance longevity.

Dr. Peter Attia emphasizes certain key nutritional guidelines throughout:

1. **Whole Foods Over Processed Ones:** We'll stick to foods in their most natural state for maximum nutrients.
2. **Balanced Macronutrients:** Carbs, proteins, and fats all have their place in our daily intake.
3. **Hydration:** No less than eight glasses of water a day, with encouragements for more if possible!
4. **No Added Sugars:** We're steering clear of refined sugars to keep insulin levels stable.

It's achievable! And remember, this isn't about perfection—it's about making better choices one meal at a time.

# Weekly Meal Plans

| DAY | BREAKFAST | LUNCH | DINNER | SNACK/ DESSERT |
|---|---|---|---|---|
| | | WEEK 1 | | |
| 1 | Banana Oat Pancakes | Simple Lentil Soup with Carrots and Celery | Herb-Crusted Roast Chicken with Root Vegetables | Dark Chocolate Avocado Mousse |
| 2 | Pineapple Cottage Cheese Bowl | Turmeric Ginger Chicken Curry | Tofu and Broccoli Stir-Fry | Edamame Hummus with Veggie Sticks |
| 3 | Broccoli and Feta Frittata | Grilled Portobello Mushroom Burgers | Sweet Potato and Black Bean Chili | Low-Carb Cinnamon Roll Mug Cake |
| 4 | Spiced Apple and Flaxseed Porridge | Spinach & Mushroom Quesadilla | Seared Scallops with Lemon Butter Sauce | Carrot and Ginger Soup Shooters |
| 5 | Spinach, Tomato, and Feta Frittata | Vegan Buddha Bowl | Grilled Lamb Chops with Rosemary and Garlic | Vegan Pumpkin Spice Energy Balls |
| 6 | Lemon Ricotta Pancakes with Raspberries | Veggie-Packed Lettuce Wraps | Stuffed Portobello Mushrooms with Quinoa and Spinach | Herb-Roasted Cashews |
| 7 | Spinach Scrambled Eggs on a Toast | Brown Rice and Black Bean Burritos | Baked Chicken Thighs with Roasted Vegetables | Almond Flour Chocolate Cake with Raspberries |
| | | WEEK 2 | | |
| 8 | Energizing Green Smoothie | Mediterranean Chickpea Salad | Black Bean Tacos with Mango Salsa | Smoked Salmon Canapés with Dill and Capers |
| 9 | Tofu Scramble with Fresh Herbs | One-pot Garlic Broccoli And Shrimp | Coconut Lime Shrimp Skewers | Chia Pudding with Mango and Coconut |

| | | | |
|---|---|---|---|
| 10 | Buckwheat Pancakes with Maple Syrup | Miso Glazed Cod with Bok Choy | Chickpea and Tomato Curry | Avocado Deviled Eggs |
| 11 | Sweet Potato Kale Hash | Garlic Herb Roasted Pork Tenderloin | Stuffed Bell Peppers with Wild Rice | Peanut Butter and Banana on Whole-Grain Crackers |
| 12 | Chia Seed Pudding with Fresh Berries | Tempeh and Vegetable Kebabs | Vegetable Stir-Fry with Tofu and Brown Rice | Spicy Roasted Chickpeas |
| 13 | Overnight Oats with Berries and Almonds | Zucchini Noodles with Pesto and Grilled Chicken | Baked Salmon with Lemon and Dill | Spiced Pumpkin Seeds |
| 14 | Quinoa Breakfast Bowl with Avocado and Spinach | Spinach and Feta Stuffed Portobello Mushrooms | Roasted Butternut Squash Soup | Baked Cinnamon Apples with Oats |
| WEEK 3 | | | | |
| 15 | Banana Oat Pancakes | Grilled Chicken and Quinoa Power Bowl | Greek Yogurt Marinated Lamb Chops | Seaweed Salad Rolls |
| 16 | Pineapple Cottage Cheese Bowl | Sweet Potato and Black Bean Wraps | Almond-Crusted Chicken Tenders | Hazelnut Mocha Protein Bars |
| 17 | Broccoli and Feta Frittata | Simple Lentil Soup with Carrots and Celery | Baked Cod with Tomato and Basil | Cauliflower Popcorn |
| 18 | Spiced Apple and Flaxseed Porridge | Turmeric Ginger Chicken Curry | Grilled Shrimp with Avocado Salsa | Dairy-Free Strawberry Cheesecake Bites |
| 19 | Spinach, Tomato, and Feta Frittata | Grilled Portobello Mushroom Burgers | Vegetable And Lentil Stew | Protein-Packed Trail Mix |
| 20 | Lemon Ricotta Pancakes with Raspberries | Spinach & Mushroom Quesadilla | Stir-Fried Tofu with Vegetables and Brown Rice | Pistachio and Rosewater Nice Cream |

| | | | |
|---|---|---|---|
| 21 | Spinach Scrambled Eggs on a Toast | Vegan Buddha Bowl | Stuffed Bell Peppers with Wild Rice | Mini Caprese Skewers |
| | | WEEK 4 | | |
| 22 | Energizing Green Smoothie | Mediterranean Chickpea Salad | Herb-Crusted Roast Chicken with Root Vegetables | No-Bake Coconut Macaroons |
| 23 | Tofu Scramble with Fresh Herbs | One-pot Garlic Broccoli And Shrimp | Tofu and Broccoli Stir-Fry | Broccoli Tots with Cheese |
| 24 | Buckwheat Pancakes with Maple Syrup | Miso Glazed Cod with Bok Choy | Sweet Potato and Black Bean Chili | Gluten-Free Carrot Cake Muffins |
| 25 | Sweet Potato Kale Hash | Garlic Herb Roasted Pork Tenderloin | Seared Scallops with Lemon Butter Sauce | Hummus with Fresh Veggies |
| 26 | Chia Seed Pudding with Fresh Berries | Tempeh and Vegetable Kebabs | Grilled Lamb Chops with Rosemary and Garlic | Baked Kale Chips with Sea Salt |
| 27 | Overnight Oats with Berries and Almonds | Zucchini Noodles with Pesto and Grilled Chicken | Stuffed Portobello Mushrooms with Quinoa and Spinach | Greek Yogurt with Honey and Walnuts |
| 28 | Quinoa Breakfast Bowl with Avocado and Spinach | Spinach and Feta Stuffed Portobello Mushrooms | Baked Chicken Thighs with Roasted Vegetables | Apple Slices with Almond Butter |
| 29 | Energizing Green Smoothie | Mediterranean Chickpea Salad | Herb-Crusted Roast Chicken with Root Vegetables | Mixed Nuts and Seeds Trail Mix |
| 30 | Tofu Scramble with Fresh Herbs | One-pot Garlic Broccoli And Shrimp | Tofu and Broccoli Stir-Fry | Herb-Roasted Cashews |

# Shopping Lists: Simplifying Your Month

When you plan your meals ahead of time and consolidate your shopping into a monthly list, you save both time and money. No more last-minute supermarket runs where you're likely to end up buying things you don't need (hello, junk food!). Plus, buying in bulk allows you to stock up on staples like grains, legumes, and spices at discounted rates.

**Step 1: Assess Your Meal Plan**

Before penning down your shopping list, take a look at your meal plan for the month. Make sure each week is balanced with a variety of nutrients and follows Dr. Peter Attia's recommendations in the Outlive Diet Cookbook.

**Step 2: Categorize Your Ingredients**

I find it easiest to categorize ingredients by their food groups; this way, you won't miss anything because similar items are grouped together. Here are some broad categories:

*Proteins:* Chicken, tofu, beans, lentils, fish

*Vegetables:* Leafy greens (spinach, kale), cruciferous veggies (broccoli, cauliflower), root veggies (carrots, potatoes)

*Fruits:* Berries, apples, bananas

*Grains:* Quinoa, brown rice

*Dairy/Alternatives:* Greek yogurt, almond milk

*Nuts/Seeds:* Almonds, chia seeds

*Herbs/Spices*: Fresh herbs like cilantro and parsley; spices like turmeric and cumin

**Step 3: Create A Master List**

Now it's time to compile all those ingredients into a master list. Let's make this practical:

**Proteins**

- ✓ 8 Chicken breasts
- ✓ 4 packs Tofu
- ✓ 2 lbs. Lentils
- ✓ 2 lbs. Black beans
- ✓ 2 lbs. Quinoa
- ✓ 4 Salmon fillets
- ✓ 2 packs Greek yogurt

**Vegetables**

- ✓ Broccoli (8 heads)
- ✓ Spinach (4 bags)
- ✓ Sweet potatoes (10)
- ✓ Bell peppers (6)
- ✓ Carrots (10)

## Fruits

- ✓ Bananas (20)
- ✓ Berries (4 pints blueberries; 4 pints raspberries)
- ✓ Apples (12)

## Grains & Alternatives

- ✓ Brown rice (5 lbs.)

## Dairy/Alternatives

- ✓ Almond milk (6 cartons)

## Nuts/Seeds

- ✓ Almonds (2 lbs)

## Herbs/Spices

- ✓ Fresh cilantro (4 bunches)

Of course, quantities may vary based on your specific recipes and family size. Adjust accordingly!

## Step 4: Incorporate Staples

Never forget to add staples to your list—those pantry essentials you always need:

## Pantry Staples

- ✓ Olive oil
- ✓ Sea salt
- ✓ Black pepper
- ✓ Garlic powder
- ✓ Onions
- ✓ Tomato paste

## Step 5: Organize Your Shopping Trips

Instead of buying everything at once—which can be daunting—consider splitting your shopping into weekly or bi-weekly trips focused on perishable items like fresh produce and weekly necessities.

✓ Start with fresh produce
✓ Move onto meats
✓ Then grains/legumes
✓ Follow with dairy
✓ Finally wrap up in canned goods and miscellaneous aisles

*By following these simple steps and ideas from Dr. Peter Attia's "Outlive," you'll streamline your monthly grocery task into an organized event that saves time and stress while contributing positively to your health journey.*

# How to Customize the Plan to Fit Your Lifestyle

So you've got your hands on the *Outlive Diet Cookbook*, and you're probably eager to start this health journey. I'm here to help you mold the plan so it fits seamlessly into your lifestyle. It's all about making the diet work for you without feeling overwhelmed or restricted.

1. **Assess Your Lifestyle Needs**: Take a moment to assess your daily schedule and routine. *Are you someone who thrives on structure, or do you prefer a more flexible approach?* Understanding this can guide how rigidly or loosely you'll follow the meal plans in this cookbook.

2. **Identify Your Goals**: *Why are you following Dr. Peter Attia's diet?* Whether it's weight management, boosting energy levels, or improving overall health, having clear goals will keep you motivated. Jot these goals down somewhere you'll see them often for a constant reminder of why you started.

3. **Meal Prepping:** Meal prepping can save you loads of time and stress, especially during busy weekdays. Set aside a couple of hours on a weekend to prep meals and snacks for the coming days.

   ➢ Choose recipes from the cookbook that you'll enjoy
   ➢ Buy all necessary ingredients in one go
   ➢ Chop veggies, marinate proteins, and portion snacks
   ➢ Batch-cook meals like soups, stews, and casseroles
   ➢ Use containers to store meals in fridge/freezer

Not only does this streamline your week, but it also ensures you're sticking to your healthy eating habits even when life gets hectic.

4. **Customize Portion Sizes**: We all have different nutritional needs based on our age, gender, level of physical activity, etc. The cookbook provides a great template, but don't hesitate to adjust portion sizes accordingly. If you're very active, consider slightly larger portions or additional snacks throughout the day.

5. **Swap Ingredients Smartly**: Don't panic if certain ingredients are hard to find or don't suit your palate:

> Substitute similar veggies if certain ones are not available.
> Swap proteins while maintaining nutritional balance (e.g., use chicken instead of tofu).
> Mix up flavorings and spices to keep meals exciting without altering their health benefits.

For example, if you're not into broccoli but love cauliflower, go ahead and make that swap in any given recipe.

6. **Incorporate Personal Favorites**: The beauty of customizing is that you can blend in your favorite foods with healthy options from the cookbook. Love avocados? Add them as toppings where possible! Enjoy spicy foods? Sprinkle some extra chili flakes into your dishes.

7. **Balance with Exercise**: Dr. Attia's diet works best when paired with regular physical activity. Choose what exercises fit best into your schedule—be it a morning jog, yoga session, or an evening walk around the neighborhood.

8. **Stay Hydrated**: Often overlooked but extremely important—proper hydration boosts metabolism and aids digestion. Keep a water bottle with you at all times and consider infused water with lemon or cucumber for added flavor.

9. **Flexibility is Key**: Give yourself grace during this process. If there's a day where sticking strictly to the meal plan isn't feasible due to social gatherings or travel plans—don't stress it! One flexible day won't derail your progress.

*Remember that this journey is unique to you—it's all about making sustainable changes that enhance your lifestyle rather than disrupt it.*

# CHAPTER 7

## Overcoming Common Challenges

# Finding Time to Cook: Quick Recipes and Time-Saving Hacks

I get it; life is busy. Between work, family, and trying to maintain some semblance of a social life, finding time to cook can feel impossible. But don't worry, I've got some tips and tricks that can help.

1. **Meal Prep Like a Pro**: Spend a couple of hours on the weekend prepping your meals for the week.

*How:* Chop up veggies, cook grains, and proteins in bulk so you just assemble during the week.

*Outcome:* Saves you tons of time after work.

2. **One-Pot Wonders**: Use recipes that only require one pot or pan.

*How:* Consider dishes like chili, stews, or even simple pasta.

*Outcome*: Minimizes cleanup time.

3. **Instant Pot & Slow Cooker**: These gadgets are lifesavers.

*How:* Throw in your ingredients in the morning and come home to a delicious meal.

*Outcome*: Hands-off cooking while you're at work or tackling other chores.

4. **Double Up**: Cook double the amount when you're making dinner.

*How:* Refrigerate or freeze half for another day.

*Outcome*: Cuts down on how often you need to cook during the week.

# Battling Decision Fatigue: Simplified Planning

You might have heard about decision fatigue before—it's essentially getting worn out from making too many decisions throughout the day. By the time dinner rolls around, choosing what to eat feels overwhelming. Here's how to make it easier:

Create a **weekly meal plan**. Pick one day (Sunday works great for most) and jot down what you'll eat each day of the week. Base this on your schedule; if you know Tuesday's going to be busy, opt for something quick like a stir-fry or salad. Trust me, having this planned out will save you mental energy later on.

Another hack is to **rotate recipes** every week or bi-weekly. Identify 10-15 recipes that you love and are comfortable making. Rotate these through different weeks so that you aren't constantly trying to come up with new ideas. Variety is essential but so is simplicity!

*Remember those recipe cards our moms used to keep?* It's time we brought that tradition back but with a modern twist—digital meal planners or apps. There are plenty out there that not only help you plan your meals but also generate shopping lists based on your choices.

Let's talk about theme nights for dinner—it's fun! Maybe Monday is Meatless Monday where plant-based dishes are the star; Taco Tuesday speaks for itself; Throwback Thursday can be for recipes you've loved from childhood; Stir-Fry Friday makes sure you end the workweek with something savory and fulfilling. This adds a sense of excitement and predictability, making it easier to choose what to eat.

| DAY | THEME | EXAMPLE MEAL |
| --- | --- | --- |
| *MON* | Meatless Monday | Veggie Stir-Fry |
| *TUE* | Taco Tuesday | Chicken or Black Bean Tacos |
| *WED* | Wellness Wednesday | Quinoa Salad with Mixed Greens |
| *THU* | Throwback Thursday | Classic Spaghetti and Meatballs |
| *FRI* | Stir-Fry Friday | Shrimp and Vegetable Stir-Fry |

*By organizing your meals this way, you turn daily meal decisions into fun, themed events.*

# How to Manage Lack of Motivation

We all hit those moments when motivation slips away, and it's totally normal. The good news is, you don't have to go through this alone. One of the best ways to stay motivated is by surrounding yourself with a supportive community. Whether it's friends, family, or online groups, having people who encourage you can make a huge difference.

I've found that joining online communities or local support groups can be incredibly uplifting. For instance, consider connecting with others on social media platforms or health forums where members share tips, challenges, and victories. It feels amazing to cheer others on and get those cheers back when you need them most.

*Here's a little tip:* If you're not feeling up to engaging with a group every day, that's okay! Sometimes, just knowing they're there for you can be enough to boost your spirits.

Now, let's talk about self-compassion. It's so easy to be hard on ourselves when we slip up or don't see immediate results. But beating yourself up won't help; it might even slow your progress. Instead, practice being kind to yourself.

Whenever you're feeling down or frustrated, take a moment to remind yourself why you started this journey in the first place. Is it for better health? More energy? Whatever it is, keep that goal in mind and understand that setbacks are part of the process.

| TRIGGER | NEGATIVE REACTION | SELF-COMPASSIONATE ACTION |
|---|---|---|
| Missed Workout | "I'm so lazy." | "I needed rest today; I'll try again tomorrow." |
| Ate Unhealthy | "I've ruined my diet." | "One meal won't undo my progress." |
| Feeling tired | "I can't do this." | "It's okay to rest and recharge." |

Remember, every step forward is progress. Embrace the journey and celebrate every win, no matter how small.

# Family Adaptations: Making the Diet Enjoyable for Everyone

Getting your family on board with new eating habits can feel daunting, but it doesn't have to be a battle. The key is making healthy eating fun and inclusive for everyone in your household. Involve your family in meal planning. This way, they feel like they have a say in what's on the menu. Ask them about their favorite foods and find healthy versions or substitutes together.

Cooking as a family can also turn meal prep into quality time rather than a chore. Kids are more likely to try new foods if they've helped make them! Plus, it's a great way for everyone to learn about nutrition in a hands-on way.

Here's an easy-to-follow chart for family-friendly meal adaptations:

| TRADITIONAL DISH | HEALTHIER TWIST |
|---|---|
| Spaghetti Bolognese | Spaghetti Squash Bolognese |
| Chicken Nuggets | Baked Chicken Tenders |
| Pizza Night | Whole Grain Crust Pizza with Veggie Toppings |
| Ice Cream Sundaes | Greek Yogurt with Fresh Fruits |

Keeping meals diverse and colorful makes healthy eating more exciting for kids and adults alike. Introduce new fruits and vegetables slowly—add them as sides or into smoothies. This makes it easier for picky eaters to accept. Plus, smoothies are a great way to sneak in some extra nutrients without anyone noticing.

# CHAPTER 8

## Science-Based Nutrition

# Fundamental Principles of Nutrition for Longevity

Science-based nutrition refers to dietary guidelines and principles grounded in scientific evidence and research. This isn't about chasing the latest fad diet; it's understanding what our bodies need to thrive for the long haul.

One of the first principles we should talk about is balance. Our bodies require a mix of macronutrients—carbohydrates, proteins, and fats—to function properly. Carbs give us energy, proteins repair tissues, and fats support cell growth and protect organs. It's like a well-oiled machine: each part needs the right kind of fuel to keep running smoothly.

1. **Balanced Diet:** This sounds cliché but it's the bedrock of long life. Eating a variety of foods ensures we get different nutrients necessary for our body's functions. Include vegetables, fruits, whole grains, lean proteins like chicken or beans, and healthy fats.

2. **Portion Control:** Even with nutritious foods, overeating can still be detrimental. Pay attention to portion sizes to avoid putting excess strain on your body systems.

3. **Hydration:** Water is essential for every cell in our body. Aim for about 8 glasses a day – more if you're active or it's particularly hot.

4. **Limiting Processed Foods:** They are usually high in added sugars, bad fats, and sodium which can be harmful in the long run. Go for whole foods instead – things that are closer to their natural state.

5. **Regular Meals:** Keeping a regular eating schedule helps regulate our metabolism and energy levels.

6. **Listening to Your Body:** Sometimes our body signals what it needs better than any diet plan can suggest. Feeling tired? Maybe you need more iron or vitamin B12-rich foods like leafy greens or lean meats.

Keeping these simple guidelines in mind helps build a strong foundation for long-lasting health.

# The Role of Antioxidants, Fiber, and Healthy Fats

Antioxidants are incredibly powerful compounds that help fight off oxidative stress in our bodies by neutralizing free radicals—those pesky atoms that can cause aging and disease. Think of antioxidants as your body's superheroes defending against villains trying to wreak havoc on your cells.

Some commonly known antioxidants include Vitamin C, Vitamin E, and beta-carotene. You can find Vitamin C in citrus fruits like oranges and grapefruits; Vitamin E in nuts like almonds; beta-carotene gives carrots their bright orange color. Including these in your diet can really do wonders for your overall health.

| ANTIOXIDANT | COMMON SOURCES |
| --- | --- |
| *Vitamin C* | Oranges, Grapefruit |
| *Vitamin E* | Almonds, Spinach |
| *Beta-Carotene* | Carrots, Sweet Potatoes |

## The Importance of Fiber

Next up is fiber—it's like a clean-up crew for your digestive system. Fiber helps regulate the body's use of sugars by keeping hunger and blood sugar in check. It also plays a role in keeping bowel movements regular (we all can appreciate that!).

There are two types of fiber: *soluble* and *insoluble*. Soluble fiber dissolves in water to form a gel-like material which can help lower blood cholesterol and glucose levels (found in oats, peas, beans). Insoluble fiber promotes the movement of material through your digestive system (found in whole wheat flour, wheat bran).

Having adequate fiber in our diet is linked to numerous benefits such as reduced risk of cardiovascular disease, improved gut health, and better weight management.

## Healthy Fats Are Your Friend

Let's not forget about fats—often misunderstood but very crucial for our wellbeing. There are good fats (unsaturated) and bad fats (saturated and trans fats). The goal here is to include more unsaturated fats which can improve blood cholesterol levels—think avocados, olive oil, nuts.

Saturated fats found in red meat and full-fat dairy products should be consumed sparingly. Trans fats are usually found in fried foods or baked goods made with hydrogenated oils—they are best avoided altogether as they contribute to bad cholesterol levels and increase the risk of heart disease.

| TYPE OF FAT | COMMON SOURCES | HEALTH IMPACT |
| --- | --- | --- |
| *Unsaturated* | Avocados, Olive oil, Nuts | Improves blood cholesterol levels, reduces inflammation |
| *Saturated* | Red meat, Full-fat dairy, Butter | Can raise bad cholesterol (LDL) levels if consumed in excess |
| *Trans* | Fried foods, commercially baked goods (with hydrogenated oils) | Increases risk of heart disease, should be avoided |

Knowing which fats to include and which to limit can help you make smarter dietary choices for long-term health.

# Superfoods and How to Incorporate Them into Your Diet

Superfoods are nutrient-dense foods that offer a lot of bang for your nutritional buck. They are packed with vitamins, minerals, antioxidants, and other helpful compounds. They often deliver these benefits in relatively few calories, making them a great choice for anyone wanting to boost their nutritional intake without overloading on empty calories. Here are some common superfoods and easy ways to add them to your meals:

1. **Berries**: Berries like blueberries, strawberries, raspberries, and blackberries are packed with antioxidants, fiber, and vitamins. These little fruits can help fight inflammation and protect your cells from damage. Plus, they're delicious and versatile.

Add a handful of berries to your morning oatmeal or yogurt. They also make a great snack on their own or blended into smoothies.

2. **Leafy Greens**: Kale, spinach, swiss chard—these leafy greens are among the most nutritious foods you can eat. They're loaded with vitamins A, C, K, fiber, and antioxidants.

Toss a handful into your salad or smoothie. You can also sauté them with some garlic and olive oil for a nutritious side dish.

3. **Nuts and Seeds**: Walnuts, almonds, chia seeds, and flaxseeds are all fantastic sources of healthy fats, protein, fiber, vitamins, and minerals. They're great for heart health and can keep you feeling full longer.

Sprinkle some on your cereal or yogurt, blend them into smoothies, or add them to salads for extra crunch.

4. **Avocados**: Avocados are not only creamy and delicious but also packed with healthy monounsaturated fats that are good for your heart. They also contain fiber and various essential nutrients like potassium and magnesium.

Spread mashed avocado on toast instead of butter or mayonnaise. Add it to salads or make guacamole for a tasty dip.

5. **Quinoa**: This ancient grain is a complete protein source because it contains all nine essential amino acids that our bodies can't make on their own. Quinoa is also rich in fiber, iron, magnesium, and manganese.

Use quinoa as a base for salads instead of rice or pasta. You can also cook it as a side dish or add it to soups for extra texture.

6. **Dark Chocolate**: Good news—dark chocolate is loaded with antioxidants! It's also known to improve heart health when consumed in moderation due to its high levels of flavonoids.

Enjoy a small piece as an afternoon treat or add it shaved or melted over fruit for dessert.

7. **Salmon**: Salmon is one of the best sources of omega-3 fatty acids which are crucial for brain health among other benefits. It's also packed with protein and other vital nutrients like B vitamins and selenium.

Grill or bake salmon fillets for dinner or enjoy smoked salmon on whole-grain toast with some cream cheese and capers for breakfast.

# Myths and Realities: What Really Works and What to Avoid

When it comes to diet and nutrition, there's no shortage of advice floating around. It seems like every day there's a new "*miracle*" food or restrictive diet promising extraordinary health benefits. So, what really works, and what should we be wary of? Let's cut through the noise and look at some common myths and the realities behind them.

**Myth 1: Carbs Are the Enemy**

We've all heard about low-carb diets being the holy grail for weight loss. The reality is not so black-and-white. Carbohydrates are our body's primary energy source, especially for brain function and physical activity. The key is choosing the right kind of carbs. Whole grains, vegetables, fruits, and legumes provide essential nutrients and fiber that processed carbs just can't match. So rather than cutting out all carbs, focus on including more whole-food sources.

*Reality Check:* Rather than demonizing an entire food group, incorporating a balanced mix of proteins, healthy fats, and complex carbohydrates will sustain energy levels and overall health.

**Myth 2: You Need Supplements to Be Healthy**

Supplements can be helpful, but they're not a substitute for a well-rounded diet. Nutrients are most effective when they come from food because they work in synergy with other nutrients to promote health. Over-relying on supplements can also lead to dangerous overdoses or nutrient imbalances.

*Reality Check:* Strive to get your vitamins and minerals from real foods like fruits, vegetables, nuts, seeds, lean proteins, and whole grains before considering supplements.

**Myth 3: Fat-Free Equals Healthy**

The fat-free craze convinced many that eliminating fat would improve health outcomes. The problem is that many fat-free products are loaded with sugar or artificial ingredients to compensate for taste. Healthy fats found in avocados, nuts, seeds, and fatty fish are essential for brain health and hormone regulation.

*Reality Check:* Focus on reducing unhealthy fats like trans fats found in fried foods or baked goods while incorporating beneficial fats into your diet.

## Myth 4: Detox Diets Cleanse Your Body

The idea that our bodies need assistance to detoxify through special juices or cleanses has been widely debunked. Our liver, kidneys, lungs, and skin are quite effective at eliminating toxins naturally without expensive detox programs.

*Reality Check:* Supporting your body's natural detoxification system requires proper hydration, a nutrient-rich diet, regular exercise, and enough sleep—not detox diets.

## Myth 5: Gluten-Free Means Healthier

Unless you have celiac disease or gluten sensitivity, there's no need to adopt a gluten-free diet. Many gluten-free products are highly processed and may lack essential nutrients compared to their whole-grain counterparts.

*Reality Check:* Choose foods based on your individual needs rather than following trends without scientific backing.

Our approach to diet should be both realistic and informed by science rather than succumbing to popular but misguided trends. By focusing on balanced eating habits tailored to individual needs rather than rigid rules or miracle fixes—sustainable health benefits become achievable for everyone involved.

# CHAPTER 9

## Sustainability and Conscious Choices

# How to Choose Sustainable and Organic Ingredients

When I started my journey toward a healthier lifestyle, I learned that my choices in food not only impacted my body but also the environment. This realization led me to explore sustainable and organic ingredients.

Choosing sustainable ingredients means being mindful of what you put in your shopping cart. It's not just about buying any organic product but understanding where it comes from and how it was produced.

1. **Local Produce:** Shopping at farmers' markets or subscribing to a local CSA (Community Supported Agriculture) box can ensure that the food on your plate didn't have to travel thousands of miles to get there. This not only reduces carbon emissions but also supports local farmers and economies.

2. **Seasonal Choices:** Eating seasonal produce is another win-win. Fruits and vegetables that are in season tend to be fresher, tastier, and more nutritious. Plus, they usually require fewer resources to grow and transport. Here's a quick look at what's generally in season throughout the year:

3. **Organic Certification:** When choosing organic products, look for certification labels like USDA Organic or equivalent certifications in your country. These labels ensure that the food was produced without synthetic pesticides or fertilizers. While organic food can sometimes be pricier, consider prioritizing items where it makes the most difference—like fruits and veggies typically high in pesticide residues (think strawberries and spinach).

4. **Sustainable Seafood:** For seafood lovers out there, sourcing sustainable seafood is vital for preserving marine ecosystems. Look for certifications like MSC (Marine Stewardship Council) or labels indicating *"sustainably caught"* methods. Overfishing is a serious problem that threatens the balance of our oceans, so making informed choices helps protect marine life.

# Reducing Food Waste: Practical Tips for Positive Impact

Food waste is one of the most pressing issues we face today. It's staggering to think about the amount of energy, water, and resources wasted when food is discarded.

1. **Plan Your Meals:** I found that planning meals ahead of time is an excellent way to reduce food waste. By deciding what I'm going to cook for the week, I avoid buying unnecessary items that end up spoiling before I can use them.

2. **Proper Storage:** Learning how to store food correctly can extend its shelf life significantly. For example:

> Keep herbs fresh by placing them in a glass of water in the fridge.
> Store potatoes in a cool, dark place away from onions.
> Use airtight containers for leftovers to keep them fresher for longer.

| FOOD ITEM | STORAGE METHOD |
|---|---|
| *Leafy Greens* | Wrap in a damp cloth; refrigerate |
| *Tomatoes* | Store at room temperature |
| *Bread* | Keep in a breadbox or freeze |
| *Meat* | Refrigerate; use within 2-3 days |

3. **Use Leftovers Creatively:** Get creative with leftovers! There are countless recipes online dedicated to revamping yesterday's dinner into something new and exciting. Stir-fries, soups, and casseroles are perfect for incorporating bits and pieces of leftover meats and veggies. You can even create your own pizza toppings with whatever you have on hand.

4. **Composting:** When food waste is unavoidable, composting is a fantastic way to recycle organic material. Even if you don't have a garden, there are small-scale indoor composting solutions available. Compost helps enrich soil, making it more fertile for growing more food.

# Eating in Harmony with the Environment

When we talk about eating in harmony with the environment, we're discussing low-impact dishes – meals that are nutritious for us and kind to our planet.

Focus on plant-based meals. Plants typically require less water, land, and energy to grow compared to animal products. For instance, producing one kilogram of beef uses about 15,000 liters of water, while the same amount of potatoes requires just 287 liters. By choosing more plant-based meals like lentil stews, vegetable stir-fries, and hearty salads, we significantly reduce our carbon footprint.

Another important aspect is minimizing food waste. *Did you know that roughly one-third of all food produced globally is wasted?* That's not just a waste of food but also a waste of resources like land, water, and labor that went into producing it. We can combat this by planning our meals effectively, using leftovers creatively (think soups or casseroles), and composting scraps.

Let's also consider packaging. Opting for bulk items or products with minimal packaging reduces plastic waste. Reusable containers and bags make a big difference too. To help visualize, here's a simple table showing the environmental impact of various foods:

| FOOD ITEM | WATER USAGE (PER KG) | CO2 EMISSIONS (KG PER KG) | LAND USE (SQ M PER KG) |
|---|---|---|---|
| *Beef* | 15,000 liters | 27 | 270 |
| *Chicken* | 4,300 liters | 6.9 | 64 |
| *Lentils* | 1,250 liters | 0.9 | 13 |
| *Potatoes* | 287 liters | 0.3 | 4 |

As you can see from the table above, choosing plant-based foods can considerably lower water usage and carbon emissions.

# The Importance of Seasonality and Local Resources

When we eat seasonally, we enjoy fruits and vegetables at their peak ripeness when they are most nutritious and flavorful. Seasonal produce doesn't require extensive energy for greenhouses or storage facilities; it's grown naturally in tune with nature's cycles.

Eating locally supports farmers in your community and reduces the travel distance your food needs to reach your plate – also known as *"food miles"*. This means fewer greenhouse gases from transportation vehicles and fresher food for you.

For example, if it's wintertime where you live, root vegetables like carrots, parsnips, and squash are typically in season. These veggies can be roasted for a delicious dinner side or pureed into a comforting soup. *In the summer months?* Look out for berries bursting with flavor, tomatoes ripe off the vine, and crisp green beans. Here's a quick seasonal produce guide:

| SEASON | FRUITS | VEGETABLES |
|---|---|---|
| *Spring* | Strawberries, Apricots | Asparagus, Peas |
| *Summer* | Berries, Peaches | Tomatoes, Bell Peppers |
| *Autumn* | Apples, Pears | Pumpkins, Sweet Potatoes |
| *Winter* | Oranges, Grapefruit | Kale, Brussels Sprouts |

Lastly, consider visiting farmers' markets or joining a CSA (Community Supported Agriculture) to get farm-fresh produce while supporting local growers. These options are often more affordable and reduce packaging waste. Plus, it's a fantastic way to learn about what's in season by chatting with the farmers themselves.

# CHAPTER 10

## Support Programs and Additional Resources

# Online Communities and Support Groups

One of the best ways to stay motivated on your diet journey is by getting involved in online communities and support groups. When I first started my quest for a healthier lifestyle, I found that talking to people who were on similar paths gave me a boost of encouragement. It's like having a bunch of friends who understand exactly what you're going through, which can be incredibly empowering.

1. **Reddit's r/loseit**: Reddit might just become your new best friend. The subreddit r/loseit has thousands of users sharing their experiences, posting progress pictures, and providing emotional support. What's fantastic about this group is its informality—people feel free to share their highs and lows without any judgment.

2. **MyFitnessPal Forum**: MyFitnessPal offers more than just calorie counting; its forum is an excellent place for finding food tips, exchange recipes, and join discussions about diet strategies. It's a treasure trove of personal stories which might just give you the inspiration you need.

3. **Facebook Groups**: Type "*diet support group*" into Facebook, and you'll find countless options. Some groups are more private and offer a safer space for people who may not feel comfortable sharing openly on more public platforms.

4. **Discord Servers**: If you love real-time conversations, Discord servers dedicated to health and fitness might be perfect for you. These servers often have multiple channels catering to different aspects of dieting—from meal prep advice to workout routines.

# Apps and Tools to Track Your Progress

Tracking isn't just about keeping an eye on how many pounds you've shed; it's also about measuring improvements in other critical areas such as mood, energy levels, or physical endurance. Through regular tracking, I discovered I was gaining strength even before I saw changes in my physique.

1. **MyFitnessPal**: First on the list is MyFitnessPal. This app allows you to log what you eat with an extensive food database that includes most restaurant menus. You can also track workouts and sync it with other fitness devices like Fitbit.

2. **Lose It!**: This user-friendly app lets you set weight loss goals and then help you achieve them by tracking your food intake and exercise. Like MyFitnessPal, it has a comprehensive food library but offers more simplified breakdowns that can be less overwhelming for beginners.

3. **Fitbit**: If you're ready to invest in some hardware, a Fitbit tracker can offer real-time feedback on your daily activities. Apart from tracking your steps, heart rate, and calories burned, it can also monitor sleep patterns which play a crucial role in overall well-being.

4. **Habitica**: If you're a fan of gamification, Habitica turns daily habits into role-playing game tasks where you earn rewards for completing objectives like drinking eight glasses of water or doing a 30-minute workout.

| PLATFORM | TYPE | KEY FEATURES |
|---|---|---|
| *r/loseit* | Reddit Community | User stories, progress pics |
| *MyFitnessPa* | Forum/App | Calorie counting, recipes |
| *Facebook Groups* | Social Media | Private group chats |
| *Discord* | Real-time Chat | Multiple discussion channels |
| *Lose It!* | App | Food intake tracking, simplified UX |
| *Fitbit* | Hardware/App | Real-time feedback, sleep monitoring |

# Recommended Podcasts and Blogs for Further Wellness Exploration

In our quest for a healthier lifestyle, sometimes we need a bit of extra guidance, inspiration, or just a different perspective. That's where podcasts and blogs come in handy. They offer free yet invaluable insights right at our fingertips. Here are some of my favorites:

1. **Podcasts**

   a) *"The Health Code" by Sarah's Day and Kurt Tilse:* This is one of those feel-good podcasts that makes you excited about wellness. They cover everything from fitness routines to nutrition tips while keeping it fun and light-hearted.

   b) *"The Doctor's Farmacy" by Dr. Mark Hyman:* If you're into the science behind nutrition, this one's for you. Dr. Hyman shares advice on how food can heal and improve our overall well-being.

   c) *"MindPump: Raw Fitness Truth" by Sal Di Stefano, Adam Schafer, and Justin Andrews:* Expect honest, no-nonsense advice on various fitness trends, debunking myths along the way.

2. **Blogs**

   a) *"Minimalist Baker" by Dana Shultz:* Perfect for those short on time but still want nutritious meals without complicated recipes.

   b) *"The Real Food Dietitians" by Jessica Beacom and Stacie Hassing:* This blog aligns well with outlive diet principles offering a variety of wholesome recipes.

c)  *"Running on Real Food" by Deryn Macey:* Focused especially on plant-based diets, it has a bunch of meal plans, guides, and easy-to-follow recipes.

# Conferences and Events for Inspiration and Learning

Occasionally stepping out from behind screens can be super motivating too! Educational conferences and wellness events allow us to deep dive into the latest wellness trends, meet like-minded individuals, and even try new things firsthand.

Here are some conferences that can rejuvenate your wellness journey:

1. **The Integrative Healthcare Symposium**: This event brings together practitioners from all fields under one roof to discuss the latest developments in holistic health.

*Date & Location:* Typically held in February in New York City.

2. **FitExpo**: One of the largest gatherings for fitness enthusiasts with everything from live workouts to nutritional workshops.

*Date & Location:* Multiple U.S. cities throughout the year, including Los Angeles and Chicago.

3. **Food Revolution Summit**: An inspiring online event where top doctors, researchers, and chefs share insights on healthy eating.

*Date & Location*: Usually held online every April.

4. **MindBody Conference**: Focused more around wellbeing through mindfulness practices; includes yoga sessions, meditation workshops alongside nutritional talks.

*Date & Location*: Annually in California (specific dates vary).

Attending even one of these events can provide a wellspring of motivation and fresh ideas.

# Conclusion

As we come to the end of the *"Outlive Diet Cookbook,"* I want to take a moment to reflect on what we've learned and how we can continue to live healthier, longer lives through the principles shared in these pages. This isn't just about following a diet for a certain number of days; it's about adopting a holistic lifestyle that prioritizes wellness and longevity.

The Outlive Diet isn't just a collection of recipes—it's a comprehensive approach to living better and longer. The goal is not to follow strict rules for a short period but to make meaningful changes that you can maintain for life. Dr. Peter Attia's guidance throughout this cookbook emphasizes the importance of balanced nutrition, regular physical activity, and mental well-being. By incorporating these easy, delicious recipes into our daily lives, we're not merely eating healthier foods; we're creating sustainable habits that can significantly impact our health over time.

Think about some of your favorite recipes from the book. These meals have not only nourished your body but have also shown you that healthy eating doesn't have to be boring or difficult. From the vibrant salads and nourishing soups to hearty dinners and satisfying snacks, each recipe is designed with longevity in mind. This diet encourages you to eat whole foods, minimize processed ingredients, and stay hydrated—all crucial elements for a long and healthy life.

## How to Maintain Results Over the Long Term

Maintaining the results you've achieved requires dedication but is entirely doable with some planning and mindfulness. Here are some practical tips:

1. Continue planning your meals ahead of time. This reduces the temptation to stray from your healthy eating habits.
2. Integrate regular physical activity into your routine. Whether it's brisk walking, yoga, or strength training, find something you enjoy so you'll stick with it.
3. Pay attention to what you eat, savor each bite, and listen to your body's hunger cues.
4. Water is essential for every function in your body. Keep yourself hydrated by drinking water throughout the day.
5. Engage with others who are on similar health journeys—whether it's friends, family, or online communities.
6. Don't underestimate the power of good sleep in maintaining overall health.
7. Keep up with regular health check-ups to monitor your progress and address any issues early on.

# Gratitude and Encouragement for Your Longevity Journey

I am incredibly grateful that you've chosen this journey towards better health and longevity with me by following the Outlive Diet Cookbook. Your commitment is commendable, and every small step you take towards improving your health is significant.

Remember that this is not about perfection but progress. Some days might be challenging, but every effort counts towards your overall goals. Keep experimenting with new recipes from the book and have fun with them; trying out different foods can make sticking with this lifestyle enjoyable rather than a chore.

Your path towards longevity doesn't end here; it's an ongoing journey filled with opportunities for growth and learning. Encourage those around you by sharing what you've learned—they might just find inspiration in your progress.

In closing, never forget why you started this journey—to live a healthier, longer life filled with energy and vitality. Here's to many more days of delicious meals and continued wellness!

# APPENDICES

## Glossary of Nutritional Terms

1. **Amino Acids:** These are the building blocks of proteins. They are vital for various bodily functions, including muscle repair and growth.

2. **Antioxidants:** Natural compounds found in foods that help neutralize free radicals, which can damage cells. Common antioxidants include vitamins C and E, selenium, and beta-carotene.

3. **Calcium:** A mineral essential for strong bones and teeth, muscle function, and nerve signaling. Dairy products are well-known sources, but leafy greens like kale are also rich in calcium.

4. **Calories:** Units of energy provided by food and beverages. Your body needs calories to perform all its functions, from breathing to running.

5. **Carbohydrates:** One of the three macronutrients. They are the body's primary source of energy. Carbs are found in foods like bread, pasta, fruits, and vegetables.

6. **Cholesterol:** A type of fat found in your blood that's necessary for building cells but can lead to heart disease when levels are too high. There is LDL (bad) cholesterol and HDL (good) cholesterol.

7. **Dietary Fiber:** Indigestible parts of plant foods that help move food through your digestive system. Foods high in fiber include beans, fruits, vegetables, and whole grains.

8. **Electrolytes:** Minerals like sodium, potassium, and magnesium that help maintain fluid balance in the body and support nerve and muscle function.

9. **Essential Fatty Acids:** Fats that the body cannot make on its own and must get from food. Examples include omega-3 and omega-6 fatty acids found in fish oils and flaxseeds.

10. **Gluten:** A protein found in wheat, barley, rye, and triticale. It gives dough its elasticity but can cause health issues for people with gluten sensitivities or celiac disease.

11. **Glycemic Index (GI):** A measure that ranks foods on how they affect blood sugar levels. Foods with a high GI can cause rapid spikes in blood sugar levels.

12. **Iron:** An essential mineral critical for making hemoglobin in red blood cells which carries oxygen from your lungs to transport it throughout your body. Red meat is a well-known source, but plants like spinach also provide iron.

13. **Macronutrients:** Nutrients required by the body in larger amounts; these include carbohydrates, proteins, and fats.

14. **Micronutrients:** Essential vitamins and minerals required by the body in smaller amounts to perform a range of physiological functions.

15. **Monounsaturated Fats:** Healthy fats found primarily in olive oil, avocados, nuts, and seeds. They can help reduce bad cholesterol levels.

16. **Phytochemicals:** Bioactive compounds found in plants that have health benefits; they contribute to the color, flavor, and disease resistance of plants.

17. **Polyunsaturated Fats:** Heart-healthy fats found in fatty fish like salmon as well as flaxseeds and walnuts. This category includes omega-3 fatty acids.
18. **Potassium:** An essential mineral that helps regulate fluid balance, muscle contractions, and nerve signals. Bananas are a well-known source of potassium.
19. **Probiotics:** Live beneficial bacteria found in fermented foods like yogurt and sauerkraut that promote gut health.
20. **Proteins:** One of the three macronutrients that help build muscle mass. Proteins are essential for growth and repair tissues.
21. **Saturated Fats:** Fats mainly found in animal products such as meat or dairy products; too much saturated fat can lead to heart disease.
22. **Sodium:** Essential mineral primarily coming from salt needed by our bodies to maintain proper fluid balance. However, too much sodium can elevate blood pressure, increasing the risk for heart disease.
23. **Trans Fats:** These are unhealthy fats that can be found in processed foods like baked goods and fried items. They're created through hydrogenation, which makes oil solid at room temperature. Consuming trans fats can raise bad cholesterol (LDL) levels and lower good cholesterol (HDL) levels.
24. **Vitamin A:** A fat-soluble vitamin important for vision, immune function, and skin health. It's abundant in foods like carrots, sweet potatoes, and liver.
25. **Vitamin B12:** An essential vitamin that helps keep the body's nerve and blood cells healthy and helps make DNA. You can find it in animal products like meat, eggs, and dairy.
26. **Vitamin D:** A fat-soluble vitamin that helps your body absorb calcium for strong bones and teeth. You can get it from sunlight exposure and foods like fatty fish and fortified dairy products.
27. **Vitamin K:** A vitamin important for blood clotting and bone health. It's found in leafy green vegetables like spinach and kale.
28. **Zinc:** An essential mineral that supports your immune system and helps with DNA synthesis. You can get zinc from foods like meat, shellfish, legumes, and seeds.

# Nutritional Tables for Key Ingredients

In this appendix, we've compiled a list of key ingredients that you'll frequently find in our recipes. These tables can help you understand not just what's going into your meals, but also why these ingredients are beneficial for you.

| INGREDIENT | BENEFITS | NOTES |
|---|---|---|
| *Kale* | High in vitamins A, K, and C; rich in antioxidants; supports heart health | Great in salads or smoothies |
| *Quinoa* | Complete protein source; high in fiber; good source of iron and magnesium | Versatile grain substitute |

| | | |
|---|---|---|
| *Avocado* | Rich in healthy fats (monounsaturated); high in fiber; contains more potassium than bananas | Perfect for toast, salads, or smoothies |
| *Chia Seeds* | High in omega-3 fatty acids; rich in fiber and protein | Best soaked before use to maximize nutrient absorption |
| *Salmon* | Excellent source of omega-3 fatty acids; high-quality protein | Wild-caught varieties are generally healthier |
| *Blueberries* | Loaded with antioxidants; supports brain health; low calorie and nutrient-dense | Ideal as a snack or smoothie ingredient |
| *Sweet Potatoes* | High in vitamin A (beta-carotene); good source of vitamin C and potassium | Versatile—their sweetness complements both savory and sweet dishes |
| *Almonds* | Great source of healthy fats, fiber, protein, magnesium, and vitamin E | Can be eaten raw or used to make almond butter |
| *Broccoli* | Packed with vitamins C and K; high in fiber; contains compounds that may support immune health | Steaming instead of boiling retains more nutrients |
| *Spinach* | Excellent source of iron, vitamins A and C; high in lutein and zeaxanthin (good for eye health) | Can be eaten raw in salads or cooked as a side dish |
| *Chickpeas* | Good source of protein and fiber | Commonly used in hummus or added to salads |
| *Oats* | Good source of carbs and fiber | Ideal for breakfast; can be used in baking or cooking |

# Grocery and Weekly Planning Checklists

Here's a basic grocery checklist that covers the essentials you'll need for most of the recipes in the book. Feel free to add or remove items based on your preferences.

**Fresh Produce**

 ✓ Dark leafy greens (spinach, kale, arugula)
 ✓ Cruciferous vegetables (broccoli, cauliflower, Brussels sprouts)
 ✓ Root vegetables (carrots, potatoes, sweet potatoes)

- ✓ Allium family (onions, garlic)
- ✓ Fresh herbs (cilantro, parsley, basil)
- ✓ Fruits (apples, berries, bananas, oranges)

## Proteins

- ✓ Lean meats (chicken breast, turkey)
- ✓ Fish and seafood (salmon, shrimp)
- ✓ Eggs
- ✓ Plant-based proteins (tofu, tempeh, legumes like lentils and chickpeas)

## Dairy & Alternatives

- ✓ Greek yogurt
- ✓ Milk or dairy-free alternatives (almond milk, soy milk)
- ✓ Cheese (cheddar, mozzarella)

## Pantry Staples

- ✓ Whole grains (brown rice, quinoa)
- ✓ Pasta (whole grain or gluten-free options)
- ✓ Canned goods (tomatoes, beans)
- ✓ Nuts and seeds (almonds, chia seeds)
- ✓ Cooking oils (olive oil, coconut oil)
- ✓ Spices and seasonings (salt, pepper, paprika)

## *Weekly Planning Checklist*

Planning your week helps you stay organized and makes it easier to stick to your diet goals. Here's a simple weekly planning checklist that can guide you:

### Before You Start:

1. *Review Your Recipes:* Look through the recipes you've picked for the week.
2. *Check Your Inventory:* See what ingredients you already have.
3. *Make a Shopping List:* Include items you'll need from the grocery checklist above.

### Weekly Prep Steps:

1. *Meal Prep Containers:* Make sure you have enough containers for storing your prepped meals.

2. *Plan Your Meals:* Assign meals to each day of the week.

3. *Prepare* **Ingredients:**

- ➢ Wash and chop vegetables.

> ➤ Measure out spices and seasonings.
> ➤ Pre-cook grains like rice or quinoa.

## 4. Batch Cook:

> ➤ Prepare bulk amounts of proteins like chicken breasts or tofu.
> ➤ Cook large batches of soups or stews.

5. **Store Properly:** Use airtight containers for storing prepped ingredients. Label containers with dates to keep track of freshness.

# Scientific References and Resources for Further Reading

1. **Dr. Peter Attia's Website** (https://peterattiamd.com): A treasure trove of blog posts, research summaries, and deep dives into various aspects of health and longevity. You'll find lots of resources straight from Dr. Attia himself.

2. **"Outlive: The Science and Art of Longevity" by Dr. Peter Attia**: This is Dr. Attia's book and it's packed with information on extending healthspan and lifespan.

3. **PubMed** (https://pubmed.ncbi.nlm.nih.gov): An invaluable resource for finding scientific papers on nutrition, exercise, and other health topics discussed in this cookbook.

4. **National Institutes of Health (NIH)** (https://www.nih.gov): Another excellent source for up-to-date research on all things related to health.

5. **Google Scholar** (https://scholar.google.com): For those who want to do a deeper dive into peer-reviewed literature.

6. **NutritionFacts.org** (https://nutritionfacts.org): A non-profit site filled with videos and articles summarizing the latest in nutrition research.

7. **American Heart Association (AHA)** (https://www.heart.org): Provides guidelines and research on maintaining a heart-healthy lifestyle which aligns well with the principles in this diet.

8. **Mayo Clinic Diet & Nutrition Center** (https://www.mayoclinic.org/healthy-lifestyle/nutrition-and-healthy-eating): A reliable source for advice on diet plans, recipes, and lifestyle tips from one of the world's leading medical institutions.

*These resources should give you a solid starting point for expanding your knowledge and understanding of the scientific foundation behind the "Outlive Diet." Keep exploring, learning, and applying these principles to lead a healthier, longer life!*

# MEASUREMENTS AND CONVERSIONS

## VOLUME EQUIVALENTS (LIQUID)

| US STANDARD | US OUNCES | METRIC (APPROX.) |
|---|---|---|
| 1 teaspoon | 1/6 oz | 5 ml |
| 1 tablespoon | 1/2 oz | 15 ml |
| 1 fluid ounce | 1 oz | 30 ml |
| 1 cup | 8 oz | 240 ml |
| 1 pint | 16 oz | 475 ml |
| 1 quart | 32 oz | 950 ml |
| 1 gallon | 128 oz | 3.8 L |

| VOLUME EQUIVALENTS (DRY) | | WEIGHT EQUIVALENTS | |
|---|---|---|---|
| US STANDARD | METRIC (APPROX.) | US STANDARD | METRIC (APPROX.) |
| 1/4 teaspoon | 1.25 ml | 1 ounce | 28 g |
| 1/2 teaspoon | 2.5 ml | 4 ounces | 113 g |
| 1 teaspoon | 5 ml | 8 ounces | 225 g |
| 1/4 cup | 60 ml | 12 ounces | 340 g |
| 1/3 cup | 80 ml | One pound (16oz) | 455 g |
| 1/2 cup | 120 ml | | |
| 1 cup | 240 ml | | |

| OVEN TEMPERATURES | |
| --- | --- |
| FAHRENHEIT | CELSIUS (APPROX.) |
| 200° F | 93° C |
| 225° F | 107° C |
| 250° F | 121° C |
| 275° F | 135° C |
| 300° F | 149° C |
| 325° F | 163° C |
| 350° F | 177° C |
| 375°F | 191° C |
| 400°F | 204° C |
| 425°F | 218°C |

*Note: The values in the tables are approximate and should be used for reference as a guide when cooking.*

Made in the USA
Las Vegas, NV
10 November 2024

11461114R00063